So I Danced Before The Lord
Eugenia Rosalie Moten

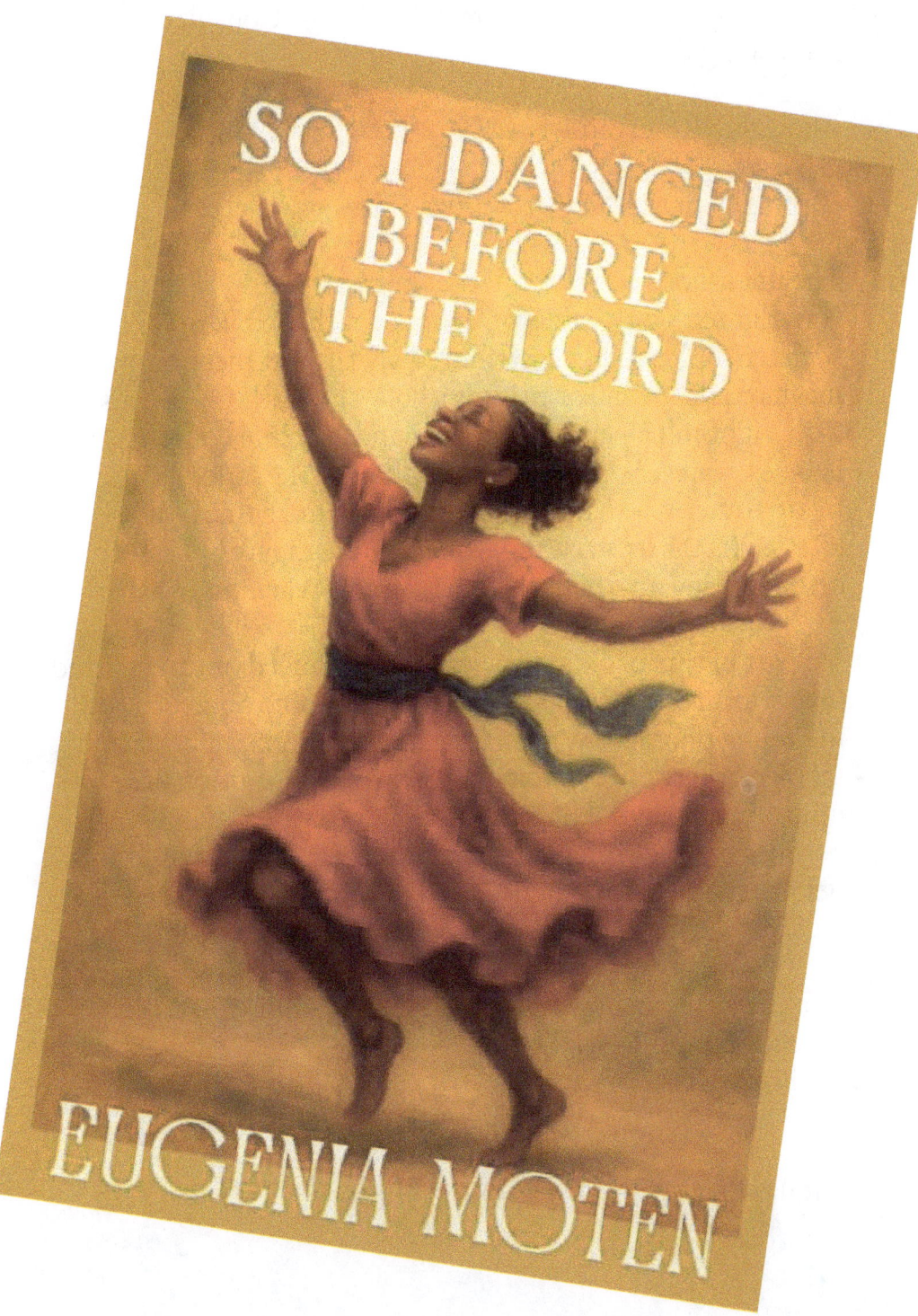

Publisher: The Crown And Cross Consulting And Publishing Co LLC

Copyright © 2025 - The Crown And Cross Consulting And Publishing Co LLC

All Rights Reserved

Originally printed in the United States of America.

The unauthorized reproduction or distribution of this copyrighted work is illegal. No part of this book may be scanned, uploaded or distributed via the internet or any other means of electronic or print without the Author's permission. Copyright infringement has legal and criminal consequences, is investigated by the FBI and is punishable under federal law by up to 5 (five) years in federal prison and a fine of $250,000.00 https://www.fbi.gov/investigate/white-collar-crime/piracy-ip-theft/fbi-anti-piracy-warning-seal

No part of this book may be used, reproduced or transmitted in any form or any means, electronic, graphic or mechanical, including photocopy, recording, taping by any information storage or retrieval system including redistribution or uploading to shared files or retrieval system without permission in writing (via certified letter only to the address below) to the below-mentioned only. In turn, you must receive a certified letter of approval back from the following:

The Crown And Cross Consulting And Publishing Co LLC
Attention: Kimberly Stratton
PO Box 952607
Lake Mary, FL 32795

ISBN (paperback): 979-8-9887391-5-9

Dedication

This book is dedicated to every person who was knocked down, stepped over, looked down on, rejected and/or felt forgotten. Why? For every time you have been knocked down, stepped over, looked down on, rejected and/or forgotten, it probably felt like a major stumbling block; however, in reality, it was a steppingstone in your life. How? You are like a rose. The more it is stepped on, the stronger the fragrance gets. So, the more you are "stepped" on, the stronger you will get. Let the negative things happen. Let the people talk. Let them be objective. Just don't get stuck there. The scripture says, *"You intended to harm me, but God intended it all for good" Genesis 50:20a NLT.*

So, get up and dance before the Lord. That's what I do. When life feels overwhelming, I dance like David danced. *"Then David danced before the Lord with all his might" 2 Samuel 6:14 NKJV.*

I also dedicate this book to my nonstop supporting, loving and caring husband, Al Moten. After 50-plus years of marriage, he still thinks I can do anything. So, for you, I dance before the Lord. Love and blessings always.

To my exceptional, loving children, grandchildren and now my great-grandchildren, thank you for inspiring and encouraging me through the little things you say and do. Yes, for you, I will dance. God has been so good to every one of you. I am blessed to have you all. And yes, you are all my "favorites". Love you dearly.

Last, but not least, I dedicate this book to you, the person who feels they don't have a reason to dance because life has been so hard. Know that you do have a reason to dance. Just start thanking God for your life and dance before the Lord.

Scriptures were taken from the following Bible versions:

KJV	King James Version
NKJV	New King James Version
ICB	International Children's Bible
NIV	New International Version
NLT	New Living Translation
AMP	Amplified Bible
MSG	The Message

Africa Study Bible NLT Urban Ministries, Inc.

Introduction
"And David danced before the Lord with all his might" 2 Samuel 6:14

Did you ever have one of those days when everything that could go wrong went wrong? From setting the alarm clock to pm instead of am? Putting night cream on your face that dries quickly in the morning, thinking it was moisturizer? Using hair spray under your arms by mistake instead of spraying deodorant? What about that one button that pops off right in the center of your shirt versus the bottom one? Stockings get a run (*who wears stockings anymore*). Milk turns into yogurt. Running late for a meeting across town, only to realize you forgot to put gas in the car. Occasionally, these are the types of days that Stephanie would have from time to time. But throughout all the drama happening in her life, Stephanie always found herself in a dancing mood. Stephanie's go-to remedy for anyone feeling overwhelmed or stuck in a bad mood was spirited and straightforward: "Honey, just dance." It was her playful yet powerful way of saying—shake off the stress, have joy and let God take the lead.

Stephanie had a twin sister, Dana, who agreed with her. Just dance your problems away. The two of them lived together, so at the end of the day, Stephanie and Dana would always fall into the house and say one of three things to each other: "You are not going to believe who I ran into today." Or, "you are not going to believe what I heard." Then there was, "Can you believe they said that?" After sharing, the two of them, regardless of how crazy things were, how silly things seemed, or how difficult the situation was, would sometimes put on music and dance around the house. This was their way of coping with life's difficulties. In their youth, they learned a song that said, *"When the Spirit of the Lord comes upon my heart, I will dance like David danced."* Their favorite part of the song was, *"I will dance, I will dance, I will dance like David danced."* So, they danced.

I relate to the twins. Growing up, I loved dancing. At times, I felt that I could dance the night away. It was a form of exercise; a time to release pent-up emotions and stress. So, I understood Stephanie and Dana. If I had a bad week in school, I would dance it out. Money got low, dance it out. As an adult, when I had a difficult day at work and was overwhelmed, I would go home, put on music and dance around. At times, if I had a terrible week, my husband and I would get all "dressed up," give the children to their grandparents and go out dancing on a Friday night. Even if it was just for one night, I exercised, released, and felt stress-free until the next day, when I had to face reality. For me, dancing serves as a means of expression and release. Britannica says, "dance is the movement of the body in a rhythmic way, usually to music and within a given space, for the purpose of expressing an idea or emotion, releasing energy, or simply taking delight in the movement itself; move in a quick and lively way." That's me. I move quickly and lively when dancing. It's something about dancing that makes all the dreadful things disappear for me. So, I dance. When I gave my life to the Lord, I decided not to stop dancing. I changed the type of music that I danced to and changed my dance partner. So, I utterly understand when some of the Saints would go forth in a praise dance or as we used to call it, "shouting." There were people who couldn't wait to get to the House of the Lord and shout until they were exhausted. Only the shouter knew what God had delivered them from. They shouted when there was sickness in the body, received a bad diagnosis from the doctor, or a child ran away. They shouted for protection, an eviction notice, no money, being low on money, demotion, promotion, being fired, divorce, or a breakup. At times, they shouted when there was a death in the family because they knew their loved one was not suffering anymore. For the scripture says, **"Let them praise his name with dancing and make music to him with timbrel and harp" Psalm 149:3.**

Why the title, *So I Dance Before The Lord*? I love 2 Samuel 6:14 because of what it means and represents in my life. I love it because David's dance was a public act, not a private display of worship and celebration of God's faithfulness. I, too, publicly worship and celebrate God for all that He has done and is doing in my life. David danced before the Lord to express his joy and gratitude for God's presence and favor as the Ark of the Covenant was brought to Jerusalem. *Take time to read the 6th chapter of 2 Samuel.* David encourages me daily to express my faith and joy in this story. It reminds me of the lyrics in a song that we sing daily in church, *"When I think of the goodness of Jesus and all that He's done for me, my soul cries out hallelujah, I thank God for saving me."* So, I Dance.

This book is for people of all ages facing problems and impossible situations that may seem unsolvable. Some of the chapters will make you smile, laugh, and at times, cry. However, at the end of every chapter, one must stop looking at the problem and instead look at the problem solver (God). Then, get up and start dancing. Come along with Stephanie and Dana as they introduce you to people from all walks of life whom they encouraged and taught to dance like David danced, knowing that eventually everything would be all right. **"And David danced before the Lord with all his might " 2 Samuel 6:14a. KJV.**

So, I Danced!

Table of Contents

Dedication .... Page 005

Introduction .... Page 006

Chapter 1 .... Page 009

Chapter 2 .... Page 017

Chapter 3 .... Page 025

Chapter 4 .... Page 030

Chapter 5 .... Page 040

Chapter 6 .... Page 051

Chapter 7 .... Page 061

Chapter 8 .... Page 068

Chapter 9 .... Page 075

Chapter 10 .... Page 083

About The Author .... Page 093

Other Books By The Author .... Page 095

Publishing Company .... Page 098

Notes .... Page 099

Chapter 1
Deal With It – Then Dance

"Let them praise his name with dancing and make music to him with timbrel and harp" Psalm 149:3

Pain is real. Disappointment is real. Hurt can be unbearable. Being excluded can cause pain, disappointment and hurt depending on the person. Stephanie started feeling moody and irritated around certain people. She felt like people were excluding her from certain conversations, activities and functions. Stephanie's emotions, attitude, and behavior towards people changed. It was not her imagination that she was being left out. A few times she even felt a feeling of rejection. But why? She chose not to share her feelings or what she thought was going on with anyone. *Why do people keep things bottled up or suffer in silence?*

Stephanie had a twin sister named Dana. For some unknown reason, Stephanie and Dana were always at a place where someone who was in dire need of sharing their hurt, pain, or even crying about how unfair their life was provided a listening ear and words of encouragement. It could be on the job, in the college cafeteria, the grocery store or at the church. When the twins were around, people felt comfortable talking to them. Strangely, though, despite feeling comfortable talking to them, the twins were often excluded from group functions and activities and never quite understood why.

After a while of being left out or not being invited to functions, Stephanie took it personally. She began to resent some of the people who had confided in her but would not invite her to their functions. Eventually, she started pretending that she did not hear people when they asked, "Do you have a minute? Can I talk to you?" Or, there were times when she pretended that she did not understand what they were talking about, and would say, "Can I talk to you later, or maybe call you?" She would walk away knowing that she would not call them. Stephanie started to become quiet towards her sister. She ignored text messages and telephone calls. Dana kept asking her what was wrong. This went on for about a month. Finally, one day Dana snapped and said, "If you are not going to talk to me, you need to talk to someone. You need to let someone help you, Stephanie. I'm beginning to worry about you." *Have you ever felt like this at one time or another? Not able to share your emotions or not wanting to talk about what was bothering you. Come on, be honest.*

Stephanie thought about what Dana had said; she needed to talk to someone. But who? Sitting in church one Sunday, Stephanie saw the name of a Christian Therapist on the church bulletin. She put the contact information in her phone. Occasionally, she would glance at the number, and finally, after several weeks of procrastinating, she decided to call and make an appointment. To her surprise, she was able to get in the same week due to a cancellation.

As Stephine drove to her appointment, she started to question if she was doing the right thing. *Why do we, in life, constantly second-guess things that we need to do?* As she pulled into the parking lot, she waited before going in. "I have a good 15 minutes before my appointment," Stephanie said. "I'll just sit here and pull myself together." She finally went into the building. "Room 210 on the second floor," Stephanie said. "I'll just run up the steps and not take the elevator." When she opened the office door, she was greeted by a cheery young man, the receptionist, in a navy-blue jacket, who quickly said. "Good afternoon, may I help you?" Stephanie replied, "My name is Stephanie and I have an appointment with Mrs. Emma Jay." The receptionist said with a smile, "She is expecting you. Please, have a seat and Mrs. Jay will be with you shortly."

Stephanie sat down in a high-backed black leather chair and waited. The waiting room was bright and beautifully decorated, with a blue-and-white theme. There was a tall water fountain in the corner. She could hear the water in the fountain as it softly trickled over the white stones. She looked around the room at the framed pictures, which featured words of encouragement. Each picture had a special message she felt was directly for her. The first one that caught her eye was, "You got this." Stephanie stood up and went to the wall to get a closer look at the inspirational quotes.

> ***"The Lord will fight for you, and you shall hold your peace"***
> ***Exodus 14:14 NKJV***

> *Discouragement:* ***"Do not be afraid or discouraged, for the Lord will personally go ahead of you." He will be with you; he will neither fail you nor abandon you" Deuteronomy 31:8 NLT***

> *Being attacked:* ***"The Lord himself will fight for you. Just stay calm" Exodus 14:14 NLT***

Stephanie whispered as she read the following one. I need this right now. Today. ***"Turn to me and be kind to me. I am lonely and hurting. My*** *troubles have grown larger. Free me from my problems" Psalms 25:16-17 ICB.*

When Stephanie sat down, she felt her left leg occasionally jumping as she waited, in anticipation of meeting her new therapist. The jumping was from a combination of nervousness and anxiety. When she thought about the reason and the different situations that led her to find a therapist, tears started to flow down her face. "Snap out of it," she whispered to herself as she quickly wiped away tears with her fingers. She picked up her black purse from the table, then hurriedly pulled out a pack of tissues and a small mirror. She dabbed at the tears under her eyes with a tissue and cleaned up the small tear streaks on her right cheek. After looking in the mirror, she whispered, "That's better. I don't want to meet my therapist looking a mess."

As soon as Stephanie put the mirror and tissue back in her purse, the dark blue door with the frosty glass top swung open. A tall lady, with a beautiful chestnut complexion and shoulder-length braids came out of the office. As she walked towards Stephanie, she extended her hand and said, "Hi, you're Stephanie, right? Nice to meet you. I'm Mrs. Emma Jay. I've been looking forward to meeting you."

Stephanie stood up, shook her hand and said, "I've been looking forward to meeting you also."

Mrs. Emma smiled and said, "Come on in and take a seat." She pointed to three chairs. "Make yourself comfortable. Pick whatever chair you would like to sit in."

"Thank you so much," Stephanie said as she put her purse on the table and sat down in a blue leather high-back chair. "Wow, this is really comfortable," she said as she pushed her back into the chair.

Before Stephanie could take a deep breath and settle down in the chair, Mrs. Emma, said "I'm glad you're comfortable. Before we get started, Stephanie, is there a particular name that you would like for me to call you? Or would you prefer that I call you Stephanie?"

Stephanie smiled and said, "Some people call me Steph or Stephie. I don't mind if you call Stephanie."

Mrs. Emma said, "So Steph or Stephie it will be. And you can call me Mrs. Emma." As Mrs. Emma settled back in her chair with a notepad on her lap, she looked over at Stephanie and said, "Most of my clients come through recommendations or by searching for a therapist that they feel has something in common with their lifestyle. You are aware that I am a Christian therapist?"

Stephanie nodded her head and said, "That is correct. That was one of the criteria on my list when I was trying to figure out what I should do or who I should turn to. I saw your card and information on the church bulletin, so I figured you were a Christian."

"Great." Mrs. Emma said. "Also, I want to point out that at the end of my sessions, I pray over my clients before they leave."

Stephanie said with a smile on her face, "That is wonderful. Thank you."
"Now tell me, Stephanie, why are you here? I read your intake form, but I want to hear directly from you." Mrs. Emma said as she looked directly at Stephanie.

Stephanie looked at the floor for about thirty seconds before responding. She finally said, "I'm here because I can't take it anymore, Mrs. Emma. I have so much on my mind. Sometimes I feel like I am going in complete circles. And, at times, I feel like I am the loneliest person in the world. I literally feel so broken." Have you ever felt like the loneliest person in the world or have you ever felt broken? Be honest. As Stephanie spoke, tears ran down her face. She tried to turn her head so Mrs. Emma would not notice the tears rolling down her cheeks, but she did.

Mrs. Emma looked at Stephanie for a few seconds, handed her a box of tissues, then she said, "Steph, what do you mean you feel so broken? Could you please elaborate a bit more? Keep in mind, I want you to speak from your heart and not say what you think I want to hear. There is no right or wrong response."

"Well," Stephanie said. "In the past month or so, I started feeling different towards people. It's because I'm so sick and tired of being left out of things. Excluded. No invites. No phone calls or texts unless I initiate the conversation. For instance, on the job, I rarely get invited to my co-worker's functions. In the church, I hear, 'we would have invited you, but we know how busy you are.' Really? That would only be after I found out about a function or gathering. Mrs. Emma, it's not only me but my twin sister Dana."

Mrs. Emma said, "Excuse me for interrupting, you have a twin sister?

Thanks for letting me know. That's important."

Stephanie continued. "Well, we are always available for anyone and everyone to talk to us when they have problems, disappointments, family issues, and the list goes on. We inherited it from our mother. She was a great listener and an out-of-this-world encourager."

Stephanie paused and then said, "Throughout the day, sometimes we listen to so many different people that there are times as soon as we get home, as crazy as it sounds, three things we say to each other: Hey, you are not going to believe who I ran into today. Or, you are not going to believe what I heard. Finally, can you believe they said that? Sometimes we look at each other and bust out laughing. Then the two of us, regardless of how crazy things were, how silly things seemed, how difficult the situation was, we put on music and danced around the house."

Stephanie couldn't stop smiling when she thought about them dancing around the house. "But lately, I stopped dancing. The more I thought about it, the more it upset me. I'm not going to lie. I got so tired of not being included in activities and functions, not being invited out to lunch or invited out to have a nice dinner." Then Stephanie's voice rose a bit. "Sometimes I want to scream because I feel so rejected, excluded, or left out." Stephanie started crying. Once she started, she couldn't stop, but she kept speaking, "God, I need help. Please help me, Mrs. Emma. I really can't take feeling this way anymore. What I am going through and how I feel is so painful and overwhelming. I wake up crying. I go to sleep crying." Stephanie could not stop the floodgate of tears that had been building up inside of her. She kept whispering into the tissue, "Please, please help me. I'm so tired. Dear God, I'm so tired of life."

Have you ever reached a point in life where, once the tears start flowing, you can't stop crying? All you want to do is ball up on the floor like a little baby and cry out to God for help. Praying that the pain goes away. Be honest. I know I have.

"I cry out loudly to God, loudly I plead with God for mercy. I spill out all my complaints before him, and spell out my troubles in detail"
Psalms 142:1-2 MSG

Stephanie told Mrs. Emma, "Sometimes I want to scream out the scriptures when I am overwhelmed or upset and see if God is going to help me. Right now, I want to yell out the scripture I heard in church on Sunday and wait for His response. It said, **"Turn to me [Lord] and be** *gracious to me, For I am alone and afflicted. The troubles of my heart are multiplied; Bring me out of my distresses" Psalms 25:16-17 AMP.*

I really like how the Children's Bible says it best: *"Turn to me and be kind to me. I am lonely and hurting. My troubles have grown larger. Free me from my problems" Psalms 25:16-17 ICB.*

Stephanie looked at Mrs. Emma and said, "I have my sister, but for some unknown reason, occasionally I feel loneliness, depression and rejection all at the same time. Even though I'm not talking to her about how I am feeling right now, I try not to let those feelings go on for too long. But for some unknown reason, I can't seem to shake this mood that I am in. I keep crying. Stephanie started crying again, to the point she slumped back in the chair.

Mrs. Emma looked at Stephanie for a few seconds. Then she walked over to where she was sitting, and asked, "May I hug you for a few seconds?" Stephanie, through her tears said, "Yes. Please. I need a hug."

After several minutes of crying, Mrs. Emma said, "I'm glad you are here. One of the greatest things you can do for yourself is to be honest about what you are going through. Remember earlier I said I want you to speak from your heart and not say what you think I want to hear. People often lie to themselves during a crisis. Or when they are facing difficult situations. Instead of reaching out for help like you are doing, they either hide the pain or go into denial and suffer silently. Not realizing that sometimes others can help them recognize and see things from a different perspective. They must trust that others can help them see things that will make a difference. So, I am glad you are here. Together, we can make a difference. Do you believe that?"

"I've learned that people will forget what you said, people will forget what you did, but people will never forget how you made them feel."
Maya Angelou

Stephanie was glad that she had chosen Mrs. Emma for her therapist. It was how she made her feel. While she was praying about her situation, she was seeking someone to help her. There were specific criteria she wanted in the person she picked: a woman therapist, on the job for more than a year or two, a woman of faith, and someone who would pray with her. She was not going to back down or take away from her list.

"Give your worries to the Lord. He will take care of you. He will never

let good people down" Psalms 55:22 ICB

Stephanie reached for her purse to retrieve her mirror. "I probably look a mess!" she said. I'm glad my sister was concerned and encouraged me to talk to someone. For the first time in over a month, I feel better."

Mrs. Emma looked at Stephanie and said, "I am glad that you listened to her. Please know that you are not the only one who feels alone in this world. For whatever reason, some people don't want to seek or ask for help. But you did. You took the first step to addressing your feelings. Now, unfortunately, Stephanie, our time for this session is up. I want to put you on a weekly schedule. What do you think about that?"

Stephanie looked out the window for a few seconds, then she replied, "That's fine with me. Because of my work schedule, Wednesday will work best for me. Are you able to get me in?"

"Yes, Wednesday's it will be," Mrs. Emma said. "Also, at some of your sessions, only if you are comfortable, I want you to share with me some of those stories or situations that you and your sister listen to. What do you think?"

Stephanie said, "Sure. I would like that."

Mrs. Emma said, "A little suggestion, it may and it may not happen, but if you feel yourself getting emotional, moody or back to where you were before you came today, I want you to do something. Take a few minutes for a little exercise and cry out to God about what you are feeling right then and there. Just tell Him as if you are talking to me. And when you come back, let me know how you felt afterward if you did it. Now let's close out in prayer." After the prayer, Stephanie thanked Mrs. Emma for everything.

Leaving the office, Stephanie almost ran to her car. Stephanie couldn't wait to get home to share with Dana how her first session with Mrs. Emma had gone. For the first time in over a month, she literally felt like dancing. Driving home, she kept saying, "Thank you, Jesus." When she pulled into her driveway, she yelled out, "Thank you, Lord." Then she ran up the stairs of the front porch and into the house where Dana was sitting on the couch.

"How did your session go, Stephie? Or would you like to wait until later to discuss it? "Dana asked when Stephanie walked in the door.

"Much better than I thought. I really like Mrs. Emma. She's so personable," Stephanie replied with a smile." I'm glad you mentioned that I should get help. I was able to really share with her how I was actually feeling regarding my emotions, my ups and downs and I also told her how we listen to so many people and their problems. "Dana, guess what? She asked me if I would feel comfortable sharing some of the different situations with her in our sessions. I told her I would love to. What do you think?"

"That sounds cool to me," Dana said. "Steph, you sound and even look better. I am so glad for you. I missed the old you. So, what's the first situation you are going to share with Mrs. Emma? Girl, we have some wild ones you can share." Dana and Stephanie couldn't stop laughing. Then suddenly Stephanie said, "You ready, sister, to put on music and dance?" And so, they danced like David danced.

Do you have something to dance about? If so, put on music and dance.

"Thou wilt keep him in perfect peace, whose mind is stayed on thee: because he trusteth in thee. Trust ye in the LORD for ever: for in the LORD JEHOVAH is everlasting strength" Isaiah 26:3-4 KJV

"Let not your heart be troubled: ye believe in God, believe also in me" John 14:1 KJV

"Pray without ceasing"
1 Thessalonians 5:17 NKJV

So, I Danced!

Chapter 2
Can You Believe That

"Give your worries to the Lord. He will take care of you. He will never let good people down" Psalms 55:22 ICB

"That rain is horrible," Dana said as she practically ran in the door, shaking her umbrella. As she was hanging up her coat in the closet, she laughingly said, "It's raining so hard that even the ducks are complaining." As Dana fell on the couch laughing, grabbing for her white fur blanket and kicking off her shoes, she said, "First of all, Sissy, I am totally, I mean totally exhausted and the day was straight up crazy. And second, girl, you are not going to believe what I heard."

Stephanie looked up from her book she was reading and said, "It couldn't have been that bad, D, you didn't call me once today." Then Stephanie chuckled. She looked at Dana and said, "What did you hear that is so unbelievable?"

Remember what Stephanie told the therapist, "at the end of the day, one of three things that we say to each other: Hey, you are not going to believe who I ran into today. You are not going to believe what I heard. Or, can you believe they said that?"

"Trust me, **you are not going to believe what I heard**," Dana said. "So, put your seat belt on and buckle up." Dana turned towards Stephanie on the couch. "Remember Wendy from work?"

"The girl who talks very softly and looks like she is afraid of her shadow," Stephanie said.

"Yep, that's her," Dana said. "Well, today I wanted to do something different instead of staying in my office for lunch, so I went outside. Even though it was sunny outside, the office building blocked the sun. I was sitting on the green bench outside the cafeteria window, eating my lunch, when Wendy approached me and asked if we could talk. I told her, sure. Stephie, she has so much going on in her life."

Stephanie said, "You mentioned that before."

Dana said, "As Wendy sat down, I asked her what was going on?"

Wendy immediately told me that her supervisor called her into the office first thing this morning. She was saying how the supervisor was talking about work production, people in the office and other things. Wendy also said that throughout the supervisor's talk, many things were going through her mind. For instance, if I'm fired, so be it. If I'm getting demoted, bring it on. If I have not been working up to your satisfaction or expectation, I can do better. Whatever it is, just let me know and stop prolonging this meeting. Just let me have it.

I looked at her and said, "Did you get fired or something, Wendy?"

Wendy said, "No. My supervisor is literally concerned about me. She said she noticed a change in my personality and pointed out that I had a few incomplete assignments. She said that was not like me at all. She also told me that she noticed, on several occasions, how irritated I became when some of my coworkers asked me a question. I am sometimes withdrawn and do not participate in the weekly staff meetings. Previously, she said I would comment on and offer suggestions for ongoing projects. Now I sit in meetings, looking down and not talking. She ended by saying, "Wendy, I am deeply concerned. Is there anything I can do or can I get someone to help you?' *Have you ever been in a situation where someone noticed a change in you and brought it to your attention because they were concerned about you? Be honest.*

Dana said, "Wendy, what did you say to your supervisor?"

"Dana, I tried not to say anything personable, but I had to. I told my supervisor about my home life and the things happening there because I think they are affecting my work and I was so sorry. I explained that I was going through so much, that I really needed this job, and that I couldn't afford to lose it. I advised my supervisor that what I was going to tell her, she needed to keep confidential, especially away from my coworkers."

She said, "Wendy, that's why I am meeting with you. To see what is going on." Then she said, "Would you be more comfortable talking to someone in Human Resources instead of me?"

I squirmed around in my seat for a few seconds, then I told my supervisor, "No. Not right now. I didn't mind talking to her." Dana, I didn't know why, I did it, but I moved my chair closer to my supervisor's desk, took off my glasses, looked directly at her, and shared my painful home life. I started by saying to my supervisor, "I would love to say that I have the best husband in the world, but I can't. I would love to say that he would do anything for me, but I can't. To say that I get incredibly excited when I hear his voice on the phone or when I receive a text from him makes me smile; again, I cannot. Wendy stopped talking for a few seconds, then she said, "Dana, I told my supervisor how I literally knew what type of man I was marrying but I just knew that once we were married, I could help change him." *Why do some women (some men) think that once they get married, they can change their mate and say, "once we get married, things will be different." Really?*

Wendy continued. I told my supervisor that before I got married, so many people kept telling me what my husband was like. Be careful. He has a temper. I didn't see it much before we got married, but shortly after, that was a different story. There's a scripture that **didn't** come true for me: **"When thou liest down, thou shalt not be afraid: Yea, thou shalt lie down, and thy sleep shall be sweet" Proverbs 3:24 KJV.** I told her, I can't remember the last time I had a peaceful night of sleep.

Wendy told Dana, I also told my supervisor, 'He is abusive, and I never know when he is going to go off, get angry, throw things or wake me up in the middle of the night to argue. When he is arguing, I go into a daze-type mood. I remember or focus on the different scriptures I have read or learned in church. They are my saving grace. I literally put them in my wallet, on the refrigerator or mirrors. One of the scriptures I focus on is *"I cry out loudly to God, loudly I plead with God for mercy. I spill out all my complaints before him, and spell out my troubles in detail" Psalms 142:1-2 MSG*.

Dana, trust me, when I tell you that I tell God all my complaints, I do. *Have you ever cried out to the Lord, telling Him your complaints and troubles? Not just a few tears, but a bucket full of tears. Instead of tissues, you needed a paper towel because the tissues weren't strong enough to hold all the tears and your runny nose. Be honest. I know I have.*

Another scripture I think about and focus on when he is arguing is *"I called out your name, O God, called from the bottom of the pit. You listened when I called out, 'Don't shut your ears!" Get me out of here! Save me!' You came close when I called out. You said, 'It's going to be all right'" Lamentations 3:55-57 MSG.* At the end of the verse, it says, *"You said, it's going to be all right."* Sometimes I would ask God when, when is everything going to be all right?

"Give your worries to the Lord. He will take care of you. He will never let good people down" Psalms 55:22 ICB

Dana, trust me when I say I give the Lord all my troubles in my prayers. I pray so much that sometimes I think God is tired of hearing from me.

Song break: In church, there is a song that we sing, *"Oh Lord it's me again. Oh Lord it's me again. I called you up this morning and I called you late last night, oh Lord it's me again." As the saints sing this song, they understand and realize they can come to the Lord as often as they want, morning, noon, or night, because He does not mind.*

"Dana, the whole time I was talking, my supervisor just kept staring at me in disbelief. I even saw her dab at her eyes a couple of times. She even asked me why I stay with him. I told her that out of the two years we have been married, he is not always abusive. He always apologizes. He always tells me he didn't mean to yell, scream or say mean things. Some people are aware of his screaming, but everyone in the community loves him for all the work that he does. But they don't really know him. Also, he is on edge with the election coming up. He wonders nonstop if he will be elected to a second term in office as a state official."

Then I told her, "I really do believe that he needs to talk to someone. He has been hurt by someone growing up. I figured that out through the things he has said to me, such as, 'You think you are better than me'. **What?** You never had to suffer the way I did. **Really**. You probably didn't have to work until you were out of school." And those are the nicer things that he has said.

I sat in my supervisor's office for an hour, mostly me talking and her listening. She commented, "I know that you are a woman of faith by the things I have heard you say, not only in the meetings, but to your coworkers." Then she asked three things, "Wendy, do you think your faith can get you through all of this? Do you love him? And do you think he really loves you the way that he treats you?"

I told her, "I trust God. So, I have faith to believe He will take care of me. And yes, I honestly believe my husband loves me, and I love him very much. But I don't like what he is doing to me. So, I do struggle here at work thinking about all that I am going through at home. Sometimes I dread going home."

"Dana, I also told her in the midst of all my struggles, even though I seem overwhelmed, act irritated and short with people, I know that someway, somehow things are going to work out."

"For with God nothing shall be impossible" Luke 1:37 NKJV

I also told her, when nothing in life makes sense, as crazy as things seem, I always run or escape to God. He will never fail me. When my husband is fussing, I hide myself in the Bible. I find strength, courage, hope and endurance. I notice that when I am reading my Bible, he walks away.

> *I will bless the Lord at all times; His praise shall continually be in my mouth. My soul makes its boast in the Lord; The humble and downtrodden will hear it and rejoice." O magnify the Lord with me, And let us lift up His name together. I sought the Lord [on the authority of His word], and He answered me, And delivered me from all my fears. They looked to Him and were radiant; Their faces will never blush in shame or confusion. This poor man cried, and the Lord heard him And saved him from all his troubles"*
> *Psalms 34:1-6 AMP*

Wendy told Dana, "When my supervisor called me in for this one thing this morning – being concerned about me but when I left her office, she said that I helped her to understand some things. I was glad for her but as for me, I still have things I need to face and deal with. I still have my husband who needs help and facing reality, I need help too. I am going to look not only for a therapist but for a marriage counselor. If things don't change, I will have to decide, do I stay with him or do I go?"

Wendy looked at Dana, a tear running down her face, and said, "I do know that I deserve to live in a peaceful home and environment."

What is your home and environment like? Is it peaceful or in turmoil? If in turmoil, what are you going to do about it?

Dana looked at Wendy and said, "I am so sorry that you are going through all of this. It does seem like you are on the right track, mind-wise, as to what you have to do. I don't have the answers. I have never been in your shoes. I can't imagine living with an abusive person but I can be available if you want to talk. I am told that I am a great listener."

The ladies looked at each other and smiled. Wendy said, "Thanks Dana, I didn't mean to take up your lunch break. I feel so much better. Between you and my supervisor, I feel that I am not alone. I still must go home, but I have a different perspective on things after finally being able to talk, I mean, really talk about what I am going through. I promise to keep you updated."

Dana replied, "No problem. You know where to find me."

If a person came to you with a problem similar to Wendy's, would you take the time to listen, or would you say, "I don't want to get involved"?

On her drive home, Dana could not stop thinking about the conversation she had with Wendy. She even said aloud, "There is no way I could go through what Wendy is going through and still live with that man. Screaming. Hollering. Fussing. No way. One of us got to go, and it's not me."

After Dana told Stephanie everything that she had heard, Stephanie looked at Dana for a few seconds, then she said, "What are you going to do about what you heard?"

Dana replied, "Right now, be a friend. A listening ear. A support unit for her. Since I know and her supervisor is aware, the key for Wendy, until she gets professional help, is to know that we are here for her. She is not alone. I am going to reach out to Dr. Stacey Wear; she works in our building, and I will suggest that she introduce herself to Wendy. She's the therapist I told you about. A lot of people who work in the building are not aware that they can talk to her."

"Alright, Sis, I know you. You are going to try to help her. Just be careful. It's a spousal thing. Let me know what I can do," Stephanie said to Dana as she threw a pillow on her lap.

Dana chuckled and said, "You know me. I sure will. Then Dana looked at Stephanie and said, "Steph, can you imagine being in Wendy's shoes? Wow, girl, that must be something."

Stephanie said with a sigh, "Can't even begin to imagine. Don't get overwhelmed, Dana, helping her."

As Dana put her head back on the stack of pillows, she said, "I won't, Sis. I promise."

"Let us not grow weary or become discouraged in doing good, for at the proper time we will reap, if we do not give in" Galatians 6:9 AMP

Abuse is real. Suffering in silence takes a toll on a person. No one should live in fear because that is not acceptable. Sometimes, all it takes is for one person to help the person suffering. A listening ear. Words of encouragement. Sitting with them. Point them in the right direction for help. Something to note, we hear about women all the time but men as well as women can be victims of abuse.

There are so many unspoken signs when a person is calling out for help. A few signs are: if you see a person's character change from happy to sad all the time, anxious, become withdrawn, have frequent accidents (so they say), wearing turtleneck shirts or long sleeves in hot weather, piling on extra makeup, jumping when the phone rings, easily startled by certain voices and so forth. If you notice something, say something. Suggest to them that they consider getting professional help. You may be their lifeline.

In a class I was taking, the instructor said, "It can take time to work up the courage to leave an abusive relationship." She added, "If you are in an abusive relationship, please talk with someone you trust who can help you and can find a safe place for you to go. She also said, if you know of someone who is being abused, share your concerns in a safe and private place. Talk to them in person. Try not to text or email them. Their abuser may have access to their phone or computer." If you or the person being abused don't know who to turn to or if you don't know how to get the help for a person that you suspect is being abused, call the 24-hour **National Domestic Violence Hotline** *at* **800-799-SAFE (800-799-7233)**. *An operator can help you/or them find the closest domestic violence center, and you never have to pay.*

An abused person may feel alone or isolated. For encouragement, the following poem by Maya Angelou *Alone* is about loneliness and togetherness. She stresses, "**Nobody, but nobody, can make it out here alone**." We all need someone to help us through the rough times.

So, I Danced!

Alone by Maya Angelou

Lying, thinking
Last night
How to find my soul a home
Where water is not thirsty
And bread loaf is not stone
I came up with one thing
And I don't believe I'm wrong
That nobody,
But nobody
Can make it out here alone.

Alone, all alone
Nobody, but nobody
Can make it out here alone.

There are some millionaires
With money they can't use
Their wives run round like banshees
Their children sing the blues
They've got expensive doctors
To cure their hearts of stone.
But nobody
No, nobody
Can make it out here alone.

Alone, all alone
Nobody, but nobody
Can make it out here alone.

Now if you listen closely
I'll tell you what I know
Storm clouds are gathering
The wind is gonna blow
The race of man is suffering
And I can hear the moan,
'Cause nobody,
But nobody
Can make it out here alone.

Alone, all alone
Nobody, but nobody
Can make it out here alone.

Chapter 3
Why Did He Dance

"Then David danced before the Lord with all his might"
2 Samuel 6:14 NKJV

You read about Stephanie and how she ended up in therapy. I'm sure we can all relate to some of what she went through. You also read how Wendy needs to make some major changes in her life. Change is good and change is necessary. Before moving on to the next chapters, let's pause and talk about Brother David (in the Bible) and some details about why he was doing all that dancing. So, did everyone agree with what he was doing? *Probably not.* Did he have his spouse's support when he danced? *You would hope so.* We understand the joy we feel when we dance—but did David experience the same emotions when he danced before the Lord? *Let's see.*

"Wearing a linen ephod, David was dancing before the Lord with all his might, while he and all Israel were bringing up the ark of the Lord with shouts and the sound of trumpets.
As the ark of the Lord was entering the City of David, Michal daughter of Saul watched from a window.
And when she saw King David leaping and dancing before the Lord, she despised him in her heart" 2 Samuel 6:14-16 NIV

The breakdown below is from the Africa Study Bible and the scriptures are from NIV.

"When David brought the Ark of God from Obed-edom's house to the place that he had prepared for it, there was great rejoicing. At the celebration, David danced before God in a way that his wife thought it was undignified for a king. In fact, his dancing so displeased Michal, Saul's daughter, that she spoke to David with disgust. She thought David should not have danced so openly because he was the king, even if his dancing was for God's glory.

"When David returned home to bless his household, Michal daughter of Saul came out to meet him and said, 'How the king of Israel has distinguished himself today, going around half-naked in full view of the slave girls of his servants as any vulgar fellow would'"
2 Samuel 6:20 NIV

Michal's rebuke made David angry because he knew he was giving honor to the Lord. He was not dancing carelessly. A Cameroonian proverb says, "You cannot hit the head and the teeth keep laughing." David was not happy when Michal ridiculed his integrity and the holiness of his God.

> *"David said to Michal, "It was before the Lord, who chose me rather than your father or anyone from his house when he appointed me ruler over the Lord's people Israel—I will celebrate before the Lord. I will become even more undignified than this, and I will be humiliated in my own eyes. But by these slave girls you spoke of, I will be held in honor" 2 Samuel 6:21-22 NIV*

So, David responded harshly to Michal, and Michal remained barren for the rest of her life. *"And Michal daughter of Saul had no children to the day of her death" 2 Samuel 6:23 NIV*.

This episode has applications for our worship and for marriage. Wives and husbands should support each other in worship of God. When spouses have a difference of opinion, it should be discussed in private, with the desire to heal, not ridicule.

In African churches, both men and women should come to the service prepared to dance before the Lord. If we are dancing for the Lord, let us do it wholeheartedly as unto the Lord. Do not resent the joy of others but support them. God loves exuberant praise."

David had an assignment that no one else could carry out, just as you and I do. God has an assignment for every one of our lives, and we are the only ones who can complete it. The key question to ask is, "What is it, Lord, that you would have me to do?" Ask Him. Get a mirror. Look at it. Take a good look at yourself. What stands out? From your experience, passion, and skills, does anything stand out? Something you are doing already is a part of your assignment. So again, what is your assignment? Stop wasting time and putting it off. Pray. Wait. Trust God. Get started. It's not about you but what God wants to do through you.

First: David's dance is a direct expression of joy and thankfulness to God for returning the Ark to Jerusalem and for establishing him as king. *Have you ever been so overcome with joy and thankful for something that has happened to you and your way of expressing that joy is dancing? If the answer is yes, then you know how David felt.*

Second: David's dance was a public act, not a private one, showing David's desire to acknowledge and celebrate God publicly.

Would you dance not just at home but also in public? How about at church, at the mall, in the grocery store, on the job or in school? If yes, there is nothing you can do when the spirit of thankfulness hits you, but dance. You don't care who is watching, what they are thinking about you, or how they feel about what you are doing.

Third: At times, not everyone will be happy for you, including your family. Prime example, Michal, David's wife. It did not say she had a frown on her face, but she despised his expression of faith (dancing). *Have you ever had a family member not be supportive of something that you are doing? If so, how did you feel? Come on now, be honest. Did it hurt, or did you not care?*

Even though David's wife didn't like what he was doing when he was doing it (and he didn't know until he went home), he had a God ordained assignment; his focus was on completing it. *Did anyone ever tell you that they were not pleased with something that you were doing? Even though they were not pleased with what you were doing, did you continue to do it anyway? Sometimes you must take a stand against what people want or think you should or should not be doing. Stop waiting for or looking to certain people for validation. If God is pleased with you, continue. Then dance.*

Do you have any Michal types in your life? These are people who openly despise you. It can be family members, so-called friends or coworkers. If the answer is yes, maybe it's time to cut them off and separate yourself from them. It is best to end those relationships. Remember Wendy in Chapter Two, who was living in a toxic relationship. She said she believed that her husband loved her. Even though she took his verbal and mental abuse *(by the way, that's not love)*, she said she loved him *(her reasoning for staying with him. Do you believe that's love?)*. The Bible tells us that **"Love is patient. Love is kind. Love endures with patience and serenity, love is kind and thoughtful, and is not jealous or envious; love does not brag and is not proud or arrogant" 1 Corinthians 13:4 AMP**. Wendy was kind and patient. She kept her abuse a secret until it started to affect her lifestyle and her productivity at work. She endured it in secret.

Also, if there are any Michals in your life, pray for them. If there are Michals on the sidelines trying to discourage you, don't allow them to hold you back and keep you from being joyful. Ask God to open their eyes and change their hearts. Then, here's the key: forgive them as Jesus has forgiven us. Forgiveness is powerful.

On the other hand, if by chance you are reading this and you are a Michal, stop reading this immediately, ask God for a heart transplant and ask for forgiveness. You have no right to look down on others and be disgusted or displeased with them. You may need to reach out to someone to ask for forgiveness and apologize for your actions. Don't think about it. Just do it. Be powerful. Apologizing is powerful. Forgiveness is powerful. Love is powerful.

> ***"I know that love is ultimately the only answer to mankind's problem"***
> ***Dr. Martin Luther King***

Back to why David danced. He poured out his heart and worshiped in the presence of the Lord. It was an expression of joy and thankfulness to God. *Can you relate to that, expressing your joy and being thankful for all that God has done for you?* Know that before the joy and thankfulness to God, there was a situation. That situation was: God had special rules for how the Ark was to be transported because of its holy nature. No one was allowed to touch the Ark, and Kohathite-Levites were designated to carry it on poles that were slipped through rings on the sides. Note that these laws were violated during the Ark's trip back to Jerusalem. Keep in mind that David and Uzzah had good intentions but disobeyed God's clear instructions from the start. *Sounds a little familiar. God gave you instructions and you were disobedient.* When the Ark was put on a cart, it disregarded its holy nature. When Uzzah touched the Ark, even though he intended to steady it because it might fall off the cart, he acted irreverently. When Uzzah's hand touched the Ark, God struck him down.

> ***"And when they came to Nachon's threshing floor, Uzzah put out his hand to the ark of God and took hold of it, for the oxen stumbled. Then the anger of the Lord was aroused against Uzzah, and God struck him there for his error; and he died there by the ark of God"***
> ***2 Samuel 6:6-7 NKJV***

David had good intentions, but unfortunately, he did not consult God's law to find out how to transport the Ark. His mistake brought grief and affliction. *We all have good intentions that sometimes lead to problems. So, what do you do when that happens? Ignore it, play it off or face the consequences? Be honest. Sometimes, I ignore it and other times, I deal with the consequences and move on.*

Things will work out. David was angry because of what happened to Uzzah, and he was also afraid of the Lord that day.

"And David became angry because of the Lord's outbreak against Uzzah; and he called the name of the place Perez Uzzah to this day. David was afraid of the Lord that day; and he said, "How can the ark of the Lord come to me" 2 Samuel 6:8-9 NKJV

David probably asked questions like we sometimes do when things don't work out the way we think they should. How do I fix this? What did I do wrong? What do I do next? There comes a time when we must consult the Lord, be still, be quiet, wait and then move forward. Don't have a pity party and get stuck. You must learn from what you did or did not do. Then, when it works out, like things worked out for David, you will be able to give God all the glory, honor and praise. *God deserves our honor and praise*. When things work out, you will be able to dance like David danced.

So, as we go into the next chapters, get your tambourine ready, put your dancing shoes on and let's:

*"Praise Him with the timbrel and dance;
Praise Him with stringed instruments and flutes!
Praise Him with loud cymbals; Praise Him with clashing cymbals!
Let everything that has breath praise the Lord. Praise the Lord"
Psalms 150:4-6 NKJV*

"Let them praise His name with the dance; Let them sing praises to Him with the timbrel and harp" Psalms 149:3 NKJV

*"Then David danced before the Lord with all his might"
2 Samuel 6:14 NKJV*

So, I Danced!

CHAPTER 4
Know Your Enemy

"For we do not wrestle against flesh and blood, but against principalities, against powers, against the rulers of the darkness of this age, against spiritual hosts of wickedness in the heavenly places"
Ephesians 6:12 NKJV

Who is your enemy? When you read that statement, you should know who your enemy is. What is the first thing that comes to mind? In life, there are so many different situations/categories in which we think a person is our enemy. The Webster Dictionary says an enemy is: *one that is antagonistic to another, especially: one seeking to injure, overthrow, or confound an opponent.* Some synonyms for the word 'enemy' are adversary, antagonist, foe, hostile and opponent.

Now knowing how the dictionary defines "enemy", let me share with you who your enemy is not (*I'm sure there are many other areas you can add to this list*). Your enemy is not a family member who is just downright rude nor the person who walks past you and never speaks. It is not the coworker who will not invite you to their functions or the person who knows all your business and you know absolutely nothing about theirs. *Nosey.* Your enemy is not the so-called friend who can't keep a secret. *Really?* The person who will never call you, but you call them repeatedly to check on them. *Inconsiderate.* Nor the person who constantly takes away from you and never gives anything back in return. Your enemy, if you can believe it, is not the person who is continually putting you down and never has words of encouragement. *Rude right.* Nor the person who causes confusion. *You must be kidding.*

The things people are doing to you and the way they are acting could make one feel that the person is **my enemy**. The key is to know **who** your enemy is. We **do have** a real enemy, but it's **not** people. When people treat us wrong, it's tempting to think of them as being our enemy. The Bible tells us who the real enemy is and what he will do. Remember one of the synonyms: adversary. That's Satan, the adversary. **The real enemy is Satan**. He wants us to view each other as the enemy rather than him – the true enemy of this world. The scripture says **"For we are not fighting against flesh and blood enemies, but against evil rulers and authorities of the unseen world"** *Ephesians 6: 12 NLT.*

Keeping in mind what I said, let's see what is going on with Stephanie. Do you think she has an enemy to deal with? If so, how do you think she will handle things?

Stephanie was on her way to her weekly therapy session when the traffic suddenly came to a halt. "What in the world is going on" Stephanie said as she was approaching the red light? As she got closer to the intersection, she noticed an accident. "God have mercy" she said aloud. She saw two cars at the intersection that had collided. The cars were so intertwined that they looked like a crumpled-up piece of paper. The vehicles were severely damaged, making it hard to identify their brands. One of the cars looked like a black SUV that had the front bumper torn off. The other was a red VW that had no passenger doors or seats. Stephanie prayed a quick prayer that no one was severely hurt.

With the accident slowing her down, trying to find a parking space and literally waiting for the elevator, she thought she would be late. "I made it right on time" Stephanie said as she walked into the office. The receptionist greeted her. "Good afternoon. It is so good to see you again. You can have a seat, and Mrs. Emma will be right with you."

Before Stephanie could sit down, the dark blue door swung open and Mrs. Emma said, "Stephanie it is so good to see you. Come on in and have a seat."

As Stephanie walked in, she noticed a beautiful hanging vine type plant. "Is that new? It is so beautiful. It reminds me of a plant my mother had in our sunroom."

Mrs. Emma said, "Yes, it is. It is a gift from a friend. I figured it would do great in the direct sunlight. Each day it seems like new leaves are forming." Mrs. Emma went over to the table near where Stephanie was sitting. Before every session, Mrs. Emma would encourage Stephanie to quiet herself by taking a few deep breaths. Then slowly exhale. Inhale. Exhale. Don't think of anything but what's in the moment, right now. Then she looked at Stephanie and said, "Well, Steph, how are you doing and how was your week?"

Stephanie looked at her and said, "It could have been better."
Stephanie started by sharing an ongoing conflict she had with a coworker named Rachel. She said that it should have ended as soon as it began if we had only talked about it. But no, we were both, I think too stubborn. We let our pride get in the way. It became noticeable with our coworkers. Trust me, I'm sure they could feel the tension between the two of us. So, I

guess someone said something to the supervisor. He called us into his office.

Have you ever been in a similar situation? You knew that you should have stopped a misunderstanding as soon as it happened. Instead, pride or being stubborn took over. Then before you knew it, things got out of hand. You and the other person stop speaking, start side-eyeing one another, and avoid interacting. Sly remarks begin along with subtle statements in meetings and gatherings. The elevator door closed without waiting for the other. Be honest. I know I have.

Stephanie told Mrs. Emma that once she and Rachel were in the meeting with their supervisor, the more he talked, the sillier the misunderstanding was. The more he spoke, the more she kept thinking, 'This is crazy.' We were friends for years. We went to church together, prayed for and with each other and spent time together. What happened?

Does this scripture apply to what Stephanie was experiencing? **"For we do not wrestle against flesh and blood, but against principalities, against powers, against the rulers of the darkness of this age, against spiritual hosts of wickedness in the heavenly places"** *Ephesians 6:12 NKJV.* This scripture says that Christians' struggles are not against people but against spiritual forces of evil. When commotion, unexplainable distractions and division come, **know who your enemy is**. So, when I say, know who your enemy is, don't take it lightly.

As I said before, we have a real enemy and it's not (necessarily) each other. Know who it is: evil spirits and/or demonic forces. The verse encourages us, the believers, to recognize the reality of spiritual warfare and equip ourselves with spiritual armor. We have an **e-n-e-m-y** in our life. One way to fight the enemy is to know the scriptures and, most of all, to love like Jesus loves. Disagreements will happen. But it is what you do and how you handle situations. Either humble yourself or stay prideful. Again, **know who your enemy is**. So yes, this scripture can apply to Stephanie.

Stephanie told Mrs. Emma, as she was sitting in the meeting, that she immediately thought about why she was not invited to Rachel's party. Why Doris, another coworker who she was really close to at one time, pretended she forgot to invite her to her son's graduation gathering. It wasn't them, it was me. Stephanie also told Mrs. Emma, the longer her supervisor talked, the more she realized she was responsible for not being invited to specific functions. In her first session, she told Mrs. Emma she did not know why she was not invited to things. Now, she realized it was her attitude. She also realized that through talking, she was responsible for not getting the promotion a few years ago because of her attitude and her stubbornness. She was asked several times to work with Rachel and Doris on projects but because she felt slighted about not being invited to their gatherings and functions, she declined or made herself unavailable. Or when she did work with them, she did not give it her full attention and was not a good team player. She thought she would be promoted, but the job was given to someone else and she was upset. She blamed Rachel, Doris and other coworkers. Even though people were still coming to her for advice and wanted her to listen to their problems, she was still hurt. As Stephanie was talking, Mrs. Emma never said a word. She kept nodding her head and occasionally taking down notes.

At times, we sometimes blame others for our shortcomings and for things we thought we should have or for promotions that were given to others and the credit that someone else received when we thought we should have been recognized. We are quick to say, "It was their fault. They did this and that to me. They got in the way." In reality, if we take a good look at ourselves, **we are our own worst enemy***. Why? Our behaviors, actions and even our thoughts can hold us back from living a full life or reaching our goals. We put things off and stay in our comfort zone. We are afraid of failure.*

"Beware of no man more than of yourself: we carry our worst enemies within us" Charles Spurgeon

I asked the question earlier: ***Do you think Stephanie has an enemy to deal with? If so, how do you think she will handle things?*** Reading what Stephanie told Mrs. Emma, she had an enemy causing division. ***Know who your enemy is.*** Stephanie said earlier about Rachel and Doris that: "We were friends for years. We went to church together, prayed for and with each other and spent time together. What happened?" What happened was what happened to numerous people, including me from time to time. We lose focus by focusing on the problem and not the problem solver. We get distracted. Yes, temporarily, we forget what the Bible tells us. ***"You will keep him in perfect peace, whose mind is stayed on You because he trusts in You" Isaiah 26:3 NKJV.***

Stephanie, per se, was not fighting with her friends and coworkers. It was the enemy, Satan, who was causing division. ***"For we are not fighting against flesh and blood enemies, but against evil rulers and authorities of the unseen world ... " Ephesians 6:12 NLT.*** The enemy's job is to keep and cause division. He will do anything to keep people from praying and studying the Bible together. There is power when two or three people come together: **"For where two or three are gathered together in My name, I am there in the midst of them." Matthew 18:20 NKJV.** That's why it is so important to know the scriptures.

Could it have been attitude, enemy or stubbornness that Stephanie was dealing with when it came to her coworkers? Remember earlier Stephanie said that **"she was responsible for not getting the promotion a few years ago because of her attitude and her stubbornness."** *Have you ever been asked to do something and because of your attitude or stubbornness, you didn't complete the task, and you lost out? And because you did not comply with a request, someone else was blessed. In a way, that is what happened to Stephanie. Everything is not always the "enemy's" fault. Responsibility must be taken. Attitude adjustment is required. Stubbornness is nothing new. Stubbornness, from childhood to adulthood, can lead a person to miss out on many opportunities and blessings. Have you ever seen a child refuse to do what their parent(s) asked them to do? For example, the parent(s) asked the child to pick up their toys and put them where they belong. The child either stands there or walks away as if they did not hear their parent(s). After numerous attempts to get the child to do what is asked, the parent(s) inform the child, that if the child does not pick up the toys, they will go in the trash. Well --- trash bag it is. Is the parent the enemy because the parent(s) threw out the toys? Parents tell the child to eat their food before they can have dessert. The child cries trying to change the mind of the parent. The crying doesn't work. The child would rather sit at the table all night as opposed to eating their food not realizing that they are only hurting themselves by getting no dessert. The crying does not move parents and in turn, again, no dessert. Is the parent the enemy? A lesson is being taught. Here is another one. A child is told to stop jumping on the couch or they will fall and hurt themselves. Refusing to listen to their parents, the child falls and hits their head on the table. This is not the first time the child has been told not to jump on the furniture. Due to not listening, the child cut their head. Is the parent the enemy for not making the child sit? Why didn't the child sit down? How about this one: a teenager/student is repeatedly asked to put their cellphone away and stop texting classmates because it is disturbing them. The teacher tells the student that there will be consequences if they do not put the phone away. The student would rather be kicked out of class and put on restrictions than put their cellphone away in the classroom. (Due to not listening, the student was suspended and deprived of after-school activities. Just put the cellphone away – that is all the student had to do. The class is only 50 minutes. Is the teacher the enemy because the* *student did not put the phone away?)* Have you ever heard a grown adult declare, "I'm going to do what I want. I don't care what 'they' say. They can't tell me what to do—I'm grown"? "They," of course, being the doctor, the law, or anyone offering sound advice. It's a bold statement, but often rooted in pride, defiance, or frustration. And while independence is part of adulthood, so is responsibility. When adults ignore wisdom, act rudely, or stubbornly reject guidance, they don't just challenge authority—they risk becoming their own worst enemy. The consequences don't disappear just because we're grown. In fact, they often grow with us. Being mature means knowing when to listen, when to yield, and when to recognize that true strength lies in humility.

In the Bible, in the book of Esther, there is a person who is rarely mentioned. If this person had only complied with a request and not been stubborn, the book of Esther probably would not have been written or written in a different way. First of all, do you know how Esther became queen? The queen before Esther took a stand of stubbornness and lost everything. The prior queen, like some of us, had an "I'm going to do what I want to do. I don't care what they say. You can't tell me what to do. I'm grown" attitude that backfired. The prior queen I'm talking about is Queen Vashti. (Esther Chapter 1)

> **"But Queen Vashti refused to come at the king's command brought by his eunuchs; therefore the king was furious, and his anger burned within him" Esther 1:12 NIV**

Because of one person's disobedience, another person's opportunity was made. People tend to forget that sometimes, out of one person's stubbornness or disobedience and refusal to listen, is another person's time for elevation and promotion. This happens a great deal in politics, jobs and even in the church.

Esther became queen because the queen before her would not do what the king requested. It wasn't because she couldn't do what was requested; the problem was that she wouldn't.

> **"On the seventh day, when the heart of the king was merry with wine, he commanded Mehuman, Biztha, Harbona, Bigtha, Abagtha, Zethar, and Carcas, seven eunuchs who served in the presence of King Ahasuerus, to bring Queen Vashti before the king, wearing her royal crown, in order to show her beauty to the people and the officials, for she was beautiful to behold. But Queen Vashti refused to come at the king's command brought by his eunuchs; therefore, the king was furious, and**

his anger burned within him" Esther 1:10-12 NKJV

Was Queen Vashti stubborn or was King Ahasuerus the enemy? There are two ways to look at it. Some might say she was stubborn, full of pride for refusing to comply with the king's request when he summoned her to appear before him and his guests. Others say she wasn't stubborn but instead, she had dignity and respect for herself. She was so beautiful that the king wanted her to parade around in front of drunken men with her crown and little to no clothes on.

Another answer is that the enemy used King Ahasuerus. Why would a person want to parade their spouse around in front of drunken men? And when she would not comply, Memucan, one of the seven eunuchs of King Ahasuerus, told the king to dispose of her. If she disrespected you, other women would think they can do the same. They will despise their husbands. *"For the queen's behavior will become known to all women, so that they will despise their husbands in their eyes, when they report, 'King Ahasuerus commanded Queen Vashti to be brought in before him, but she did not come" Esther 1:17 NKJV.*

Since Queen Vashti did not do what was required of her, someone else had to step in. That someone else was, after the process of elimination and preparation, was Queen Esther. God's plan all along was for Esther to be queen. He knew the sacrifices she would make. He knew that she would have to stand in the gap for her people. He knew, when it was all said and done, that she would be victorious.

Truth be told, Queen Vashti was not stubborn. She was a woman of dignity and she did not want to be on display when the king summoned her to his feast or banquet. But according to God's plan, she was not to stay queen even though she was married to the king. She was, as I call it, on a 'temporary assignment'. Queen Vashti was not assigned to help rescue the Jewish people from death. The famous line quoted was never hers: "If I perish, I perish" (Esther 4:16b NKJV). Those were Queen Esther lines. That was Queen Esther's story.

Like Queen Vashti, change will come if one does not comply with the request of the leader. In this case, it was the king. There is usually a penalty to pay. The person sometimes making the request will give several opportunities for the person to do what is required. After a while, the requester will assume that the person is not going to comply and then, a change must occur.

Be honest. How many times have you missed out on something because you were stubborn, prideful, had a bad attitude, or blamed others? Makes you think.

After Stephanie was done sharing with Mrs. Emma, she felt tears running down her face. She looked at Mrs. Emma and said, "I did not realize that I was responsible for the way Rachel, Doris and some of the coworkers were feeling towards me until I said it aloud. My attitude, wow. For a long time, I was focusing on how I thought they were making me feel and I lost track of how they may have been feeling. I blamed everyone else and accused them of something I did to myself. Kindness and compassion keep ringing in my ears and in my heart. After talking, I can say that I feel like a weight has been lifted off my shoulders."

"And be kind to one another, tenderhearted, forgiving one another, even as God in Christ forgave you" Ephesians 4:32 NKJV

Mrs. Emma said, "Stephanie today you made a great deal of progress. You took some big steps getting towards your goal and recognizing that things are not always the way they seem. When your sister noticed you were changing, getting upset and you would not talk to her, she was concerned about you and she did the right thing suggesting that you get some help. I'm glad you listened to her. Well, that about does it for today." Mrs. Emma then closed the session in prayer.

Forgiveness: When Stephanie got in her car, a song came on the radio that made her cry. The words were from one of her favorite Bible verses, *"I will lift up mine eyes to the hills from whence cometh my help"*. As soon as the song got to "my help" a flood gate of tears poured down Stephanie's face. As she sat in her car in the parking lot, unable to drive due to the tears, she prayed to God to please forgive her for not coming to Him first with her problems. Forgive her for not trusting Him to work things out and to forgive her for how she had treated Rachel, Doris and her coworker. She asked God to forgive her for not realizing that it was not others, but instead it was her. As she prayed, she could not stop crying. Repeatedly, she kept saying, "Forgive me, Lord. Forgive me Lord. Forgive me. Teach me continuously how to forgive others." *Have you ever been broken like this, just crying out to God for forgiveness? I have on numerous occasions and I'm sure there will be other times in the future. There is healing in forgiving and peace in forgiving. We serve a forgiving and just God.*

"For if you forgive men their trespasses, your heavenly Father will also

forgive you" Matthew 6:14 NKJV

As Stephanie reached for the tissue box on the passenger seat, she started thanking God. She thanked Him for using the therapist, for her supervisor calling her into his office, for showing her herself and before she pulled out of the parking lot, she thanked Him for the reminder in the song on the radio, *"I will lift up mine eyes".*

"I will lift up my eyes to the hills from whence comes my help? My help comes from the Lord, who made heaven and earth"
Psalms 121:1-2 NKJV

How many times have you gotten into your car and a song came on the radio and all you could do was give God praise? Or how many times have you stayed in a parking lot or sat in your driveway just thanking God for all that He has brought you through? I lost count a long time ago.

Stephanie could not wait to share with Dana how her session went. She felt like the weight of the world was lifted off her shoulders. "I guess this is what therapy is all about," Stephanie said.

Closing Fact: It is so important to know who your enemy is. Once you know who your enemy is, then you can start to have peace and understand: ***"These things I have spoken to you, that in Me you may have peace. In the world you will have tribulation; but be of good cheer, I have overcome the world" John 16:33 NKJV.***

Then you will be able to confidently do what Psalm says, *"I will lift up mine eyes unto the hills, From whence cometh my help. My help cometh from the LORD, Which made heaven and earth. He will not suffer thy foot to be moved: He that keepeth thee will not slumber. Behold, he that keepeth Israel Shall neither slumber nor sleep. The LORD is thy keeper: The LORD is thy shade upon thy right hand. The sun shall not smite thee by day, Nor the moon by night. The LORD shall preserve thee from all evil: He shall preserve thy soul. The LORD shall preserve thy going out and thy coming in From this time forth, and even for evermore"* **Psalm 121:1-8 KJV.**

A praise dance song that comes to mind is *"When I think of His goodness and all He's done for me. When I think of His goodness and how he set me free I can dance, dance, dance, all night."* I'm literally picturing the Saints going forth in praise and dance for the Lord.

"Then David danced before the Lord with all his might"
2 Samuel 6:14 NKJV

So, I Danced!

CHAPTER 5
When Things Are Out Of Place, What Do You Do

"I will lift up mine eyes unto the hills from whence cometh my help. My help cometh from the Lord" Psalm 121:1

When things are out of place, what do you do? When things are not where you thought you put them, how do you feel? The average person would do one or two things. Stop what they are doing and put things back in order or search for the missing object. When a person puts something down, (like me), they like to go back and get it right where they thought they left it. Right? But if by chance, when they go back to pick up the item, sometimes they tend to get frustrated, overwhelmed, upset or concerned because the item is not where they thought they left it especially if they are looking for their keys when they are in a rush, their cell phone to make a call, or perhaps their wallet to pay for a delivery. Have you ever had one of those days where you put something down, you went to the last place you thought it was and could not find it? What do you do?

On a Sunday morning, Dana was having one of those days. Stephanie yelled from her room, "Dana, are you almost ready? We're going to have to leave soon. This is Youth Sunday, and you know how all the extras come to church to see their little ones sing and participate in the program. And girl you know how hard it can be trying to get a seat towards the front."

Dana replied, "Give me a few more minutes. I'll meet you downstairs." Then Dana whispered under her breath, "If I can find something that fits." After shuffling through the closet one more time, Dana pulled out her old faithful dress, as she called it. "Yep, this is it. Lady blue and green, you get to go to church again" she chuckled as she pulled the dress out of the closet and slipped it over her head. Then she grabbed a black pair of shoes from a box on the top shelf and a matching purse hanging on the door. "Looks good to me," Dana said as she glanced in the mirror walking out of her bedroom. "Ready, Sis," she said as she dashed towards the door. On their way to church, Stephanie said, "I wonder if Aunt Trudy will be there? The only time she really comes to church is when the Youth Ministry is in charge and that's on the fifth Sunday."

Dana laughed. "Aunt Trudy says that it's the 'In and Out' Service. Youth get you in and before you know it, you're on your way out. They keep the service moving. As long as the adults stay out of their way." That's Aunty for you.

I don't know about you, but I love it when the young people are in charge of the service. I love to see them praise and worship the Lord on their level. What I love most is that they are innocent and downright genuine. I may be taking it out of context, but I love the different scriptures that say, "to suffer the little children to come unto me." Don't stop them. Let them come to Jesus just as they are. Hallelujah! I look at the scripture, "Suffer the little children as they are not adults, but their childlike faith and openness to God will be rewarded". God knows their heart. Let them come as children and youth and praise the Lord in their own way.

"But Jesus said, Suffer little children, and forbid them not, to come unto me: for of such is the kingdom of heaven"
Matthew 19:14 KJV

"But when Jesus saw it, he was much displeased, and said unto them, Suffer the little children to come unto me, and forbid them not: for of such is the kingdom of God" Mark 10:14 KJV

"But Jesus called them unto him, and said, Suffer little children to come unto me, and forbid them not: for of such is the kingdom of God"
Luke 18:16 KJV

In the scripture passages from Matthew, Mark, and Luke, it is important to understand why Jesus told his followers to allow the little children to come to Him. He was instructing His disciples to welcome children and not turn them away. The children were not out of place; rather, the disciples seemed to try to prevent them from approaching Jesus. They probably saw the children as a distraction. If you consider it, Jesus rebuked the disciples because He explicitly told them to let the children come. I'm sure the children standing there felt special when Jesus invited them to come to Him. These are not the only scriptures where Jesus mentioned and emphasized the importance of children. The following scripture:

At that time the disciples came to Jesus and asked, "Who, then, is the greatest in the kingdom of heaven?" He called a little child to him, and placed the child among them. And he said: "Truly I tell you, unless you change and become like little children, you will never enter the kingdom of heaven. Therefore, whoever takes the lowly position of this child is the greatest in the kingdom of heaven"
Matthew 18:1-4 NIV

In the above scripture, the disciples were focusing on who would be the greatest. *What is up with those disciples?* Jesus let them know unless you become like little children, you will never enter the kingdom of heaven. This is also saying that you cannot make it into the kingdom of God on worldly power, or your status, but a childlike trust in God. The key here Jesus was not telling them to be childish or immature, but to humble themselves like a child. To be trusting, teachable, have simplicity, don't act like you are so important, in a higher class and better than others attitude. *The above was taken from the mind of Genia Moten.* Also, I want to point out that God loves children and they are precious to Him. That is why He is so protective of them. I love the following:

> ***"And whoever welcomes one such child in my name welcomes me. If anyone causes one of these little ones—those who believe in me—to stumble, it would be better for them to have a large millstone hung around their neck and to be drowned in the depths of the sea" Matthew 18:5-6 NIV***

Always take the time to let children and youth know how special and precious they are. Everyone needs encouragement from time to time, especially children.

"As always, the youth did an excellent job. The praise dance and the youth choir were outstanding. They almost made me want to jump up into the choir stand and sing with them," Stephanie said, laughing as she was walking out the church door towards her car.

Dana said jokingly, "I think I want to join the Youth Praise Dance Team. I like those beautiful flags. What a way to praise God with those flags. My goodness, they were great. I couldn't handle being on the Adult Praise Dance Team. That would be too much for me. They would kick me out after the first rehearsal."

As the girls were walking and laughing, suddenly, they heard, "What a wonderful In and Out service," Aunt Trudy said as she grabbed Dana and Stephanie together by the shoulders and kissed each one of them on the cheek. "Love you. And, love you." As always, she was in a rush. As she was running towards her car, she yelled over her shoulder her usual "don't be a stranger. You two know where I live. The address hasn't changed. Your keys still work. Food in the Fridge. Love you more. Bye."

"One of these days Aunt Trudy is going to actually meet some of the people personally," Dana said laughing. "She is always in a rush. She is just like Dad. Running."

"Aunt Trudy told me that if she sticks around after church, she will be asked to do something she doesn't want to be bothered with. She said she served her sentence years ago working ninety jobs in the church. I'm too old to be bothered with this church stuff. I come, sit, listen, learn and leave. You younger people can do it now. It's your time to work," Stephanie said in her aunt's tone of voice as they were walking towards the car. "That's our Aunt Trudy. One of a kind," she added.

"You ready to go home? I want to take all these clothes off, eat, sit down and take it easy for the rest of the day," Dana said.

"You know that's right. I totally agree with everything that came out of your mouth," Stephanie said laughing.

At home, as Stephanie and Dana were sitting on the couch, they started talking about the sermon. "The Youth Pastor, Pastor Sandy, did an excellent job preaching about the Prodigal Son. I love how her focus was not on the father, but on how the mother was feeling. Kinda reminded me of Daniel and what happened in their family about three years ago with their son David except there was no inheritance involved, just a runaway child looking for answers," Stephanie said.

David was furious when he saw the list of players on the roster for the basketball team and who the head and assistant Captain were. Also, his name was at the bottom of the roster as if it were put on at the last minute. "What. This has to be a joke" he thought. He quickly took out his cellphone and took a picture. "I can't wait for Dad to see this" he whispered to himself. "As hard as I have been working, this is so unfair. Something is not right. This is wack. I deserve to be captain," he said. David left the gym and ran up the hall to his next class.

Daniel, David's father, was just leaving the supermarket when he saw the picture of the team's roster in a text from his son. "What? This is crazy. Really crazy. David deserves to be at least one of the captains" he said aloud. As he was walking towards his car furious. Then he saw Stephanie, a friend of the family, putting groceries in her car.

"Step, let me help you with that" Daniel said.

"Thanks Dan" Stephanie replied.

Before she could ask him how his wife and family were doing, Daniel went into a full outright rage about how unfair the new coach was at the High School. Then, how committed and faithful his son has been to the team. Preparing and practicing for long hours. Now a new coach comes in with a new agenda and changes everything. "My son should be the number one player. My son has been consistent and dedicated more than anybody else. And he was added to the list like he was a nobody. Just another player. Stephie, that's so wrong," Daniel said. "That's just downright wrong" he repeated twice.

Stephanie looked at Daniel for a few seconds. "Well, I don't need to ask what's new with the family," she said jokingly.

"Sorry Steph. I'm just upset. My son has worked so hard for the team. As the old saying goes, he used his blood, sweat and tears to do his best for the team. Now, in his last year, he's getting kicked to the curb by a new coach and not even being recognized as an outstanding player" Daniel said.

Before Stephanie could say anything, Daniel said "and don't let me get started on my wife. When I tell her how unfair this is for our son, Steph, you know her by now what she will say. 'Let's pray about it. There is something that God is trying to teach us through this.' Look I believe in prayer like the next person, but my wife takes things to a whole new level. She never stops."

"Pray without ceasing" 1 Thessalonians 5:17 NKJV

Stephanie was able to get in, "I know she is a praying woman and she truly trusts and believes in God."

"She sure does," Daniel said sharply. "She sure does." Then he paused for a few seconds and said, "Remember when our son David ran away. He was gone for four whole weeks. I couldn't eat, sleep and I could barely go to work. I kept looking out the window, looking for a police car to pull up in the drive any moment to give us an update. I kept checking my phone to make sure it was charged or that I hadn't missed a call. I was a total wreck, Steph."

"You sure were," Steph said. "I remember that time very well. We were all supportive and went through it with you and the family."

"But my wife was a true champ. This woman cried a little at first.

Called all his friends, family, the school, and the police and whoever else she could call. We looked everywhere for him. Then she started praying nonstop. Morning, noon and night. She said she trusted and believed that he was all right, and God was watching over him. It was on the News and everything. Everything seemed to be out of order. I mean everything. But my wife did not see things that way. I kept asking her, 'What do we do?' 'Trust and believe God because He will work things out'. Yep, she said that in all our prayer sessions with her," Stephanie said. "And what happened Daniel? Your son finally came home. True what he did was wrong and how he left, but eventually he came back home. He had to realize on his own that he had made a mistake. Running off with those other two boys and not talking to you and your wife about his feelings was wrong and he sees that now."

"I know he finally came home, but when he was gone, man I was devastated. But he knew that he was wrong too. He shared in our therapy sessions what he went through on the streets at night. He said he was scared to death and sometimes they had nothing to eat or drink. No place to bathe or shower, nothing. I almost cried. I asked him several times in the session and when we were alone, why he didn't come home? He said he knew we were angry with him and that he was afraid. He also said he didn't want the boys to make fun of him and call him a baby for wanting to go back home. But he was really glad when the police picked them up in that dirty, broken-down abandoned building. He said he was never so happy to see the police. He knew that was his ticket home."

Daniel stopped talking for a few seconds then said, "My wife never lost hope. She trusted and believed that God would bring him back and He did. That was almost three years ago. He has been doing so well but it feels like he still must prove himself to people. Every now and then, people – like his coach – will mention what he did. David told me a couple of times that the coach told him he had to stay focused. When things go wrong, he can't run away. Running away never solves anything. My son hated that statement. Running away. So, he messed up. We forgave him. Others must let things go and not hold it over his head. He has been in therapy for close to three years, which is a blessing. Now this. It just isn't fair, Steph. He deserves to at least be one of those captains."

"Daniel, I hear what you are saying but go home and talk to your wife. Indeed, it's not fair, but this time I am on the side of the praying woman. Dan, I have a feeling something is going to work out. Also, talk to your son. Who knows what God has in store for him? Help him to see that. Tell him to try not to dwell on the negative and what he didn't get right now.

But on the positive side, what God has for him, he is going to receive," Stephanie said.

Have you ever been at a time in your life when you felt like you had been totally overlooked? Had those "are you kidding me" feelings and thoughts? What about a that's not fair kind of attitude? Or, why not me type of feelings. Be honest. At one time or another, I know I have. If your answer is yes, you can relate to how David felt when he saw the basketball roster. How did you overcome those feelings? Did you wallow for days, go into a period of depression, bend the ear of anyone that would listen and feel sorry for you, or did you stop, drop, and pray? Hopefully, you committed the situation over to God.

As Stephanie was getting in her car, she said, "Daniel as a father your job is to teach your son that everything he thinks he should have will not always happen. If something is the will of the Lord, then it will be. That song we sing, *"What God had for me it is for me,"* is true. Remember the words say: *"What God has for me, it is for me. What God has for me, it is for me. I know without a doubt that He will work it out. What God has for me it is for me."* Be a good example by showing that disappointments will come, but trust that God never makes a mistake. When you pick him up, let him blow off steam, then not only talk to him but pray with him. David wants to see your reactions, his father. This is a great teaching moment. Stay calm, listen to him, give guidance and tell him to thank God for allowing him to be healthy and able to play basketball. Then pray together. Go home and share with your wife. I honestly believe God is not only trying to teach your son something but you as well."

Daniel said, "I didn't look at it that way. You are right, I must stay calm. David seems to mirror my reactions to things. My God you are so right Steph. You are so right. God planned for me to see you before I picked up David. Man, I was hot when I saw what happened to my son but talking to you, I see where God ordained this meeting of me running into you. Look at God. He's in total control of our lives. Wow. I feel much better now. I must run and pick up David from school now. Gotta go. Tell Dana hi for me."

Has that ever happened to you? You ran into someone whom you thought was by accident and walked away totally blessed. I know for a fact I have numerous times. That's a God ordained "run-in."

Before Stephanie and Daniel drove off, Stephanie said a quick prayer over Daniel and David's meeting and for continued peace in their home. Daniel thanked her again and left.

> *"Pray without ceasing"* 1 Thessalonians 5:17 NKJV

Dana looked at Stephanie, "You know you are right. I remember when David left. His mother was overwhelmed at first, but it was his father, Daniel, who took things extremely hard. Wow, it sounds sort of like the message of this morning but with a different twist. The sermon focused on the mother rather than the father. I love Pastor Sandy's topic, ***"When things or people are out of place, what do you do?"*** Dana said. I just loved it.

Stephanie said, "I liked her introduction when she said, "Sorry men, I'm not focusing on you today, the fathers, but I'm focusing on the mother of the prodigal son." I've never heard anyone talk about the mother. When Pastor Sandy said, "It must have been excruciating for a mother to watch her son leave." Could you imagine Daniel's wife? Not that she saw David leave, he ran away. You know what, Dana? The prodigal son's mother knew her son was defiant and rebellious. Daniel said something that caught my ear when he said the family was in therapy. So, some stuff was going on in that house. A child is not going to just up and run away for no reason."

"I totally agree," Dana said. "You are right, though; the prodigal son's mother knew that the boy was strong-willed and rude. Especially when he told his father "I want my share of your estate now before you die." So, the father agreed and gave it to him. Really. Not in today's society. I think things would have been a whole lot different. Remember what Pastor Sandy said, "this wasn't a surprise to the mother due to his attitude but a part of her wanted to protect and shelter her son and not allow him to leave". She was probably one of those mothers who would walk through fire to keep him safe. I'm sure it took all the strength and love she could muster to let him go. One of the key points she made is that 'even loving someone means letting them walk away. Allowing them to learn life lessons for themselves'."

> *"Then He said: "A certain man had two sons. And the younger of them said to his father, 'Father, give me the portion of goods that falls to me.' So, he divided to them his livelihood. And not many days after, the younger son gathered all together, journeyed to a far country, and there wasted his possessions with prodigal living"* Luke 15:11-13 NKJV

Stephanie said, "Pastor Sandy also said, sometimes you have to realize as a parent, you have done all that you can to help your children. Then it is up to them. However, when the prodigal son made up his mind to leave, I'm sure this mother's heart felt like heavy bricks when he did go. She probably wondered if she would ever see him alive again."

Dana sat on the end of the couch and said, "I can still hear Pastor Sandy say as her voice started to escalate, "like any good mother, I'm sure she prayed. I'm sure, like all moms —because I'm a mom too —in times of trouble, this mother cried out to God with groans. That type of groans that only the Holy Spirit could decipher."

"Stephanie, Dana said, "can you imagine being the prodigal son's mother, and in the midst of all that she was going through, she still had to take care of the rest of her family because that's what women do. We don't stop. We keep going on. I'm sure she continued to trust God but Girl, the pain and loss of not knowing where her son was after he left, I'm sure it took a toll on her."

Stephanie said, "Also, try to imagine each morning how difficult it was for her to get out of bed. Can you see her brushing her hair? You know they had really long hair in biblical times, and pieces of it would come out in the brush. I'm trying to picture her the way Pastor Sandy said. She probably cooked meals for her family even though she didn't want to eat by herself. Breaking out in hives on her skin that showed the stress, knowing her boy was somewhere out in the world. But somehow, she managed to put one foot in front of the other, never forgetting her son."

Dana said, "I think like Daniel's wife, in the back of her mind, never gave up hope that she would see David, like the prodigal son's mother never gave up hope she would see her son again. Didn't you say that Daniel's wife is a praying woman? Cause I don't know her like that. If so, I'm sure that's why she seemed calm to Daniel, but if he took a good look at his wife, he probably would have seen that her pillow was often wet from tears when she cried herself to sleep because that's what moms do."

Stephanie said, "I heard so many people agree with Pastor Sandy when she said, 'Let's be honest. The prodigal son's mother, like so many other mothers, when children are out of place and things happen, probably questions their parenting skills. Some even go so far as to take scripture and put it in question form'". *Have you ever done that? I know I have taken a scripture and made it my own question such as:* ***"Why art thou cast down, O my sour? And why art thou disquieted within me? Hope thou in God; for I shall yet praise him, who is the health of my*** *countenance, and my God Psalm 42:11 KJV.*

Another version: *"Why am I so sad? Why am I so upset? I should put my hope in God. I should keep praising him, my Savior and my God" Psalm 42:11 ICB.*

Stephanie also said, "Pastor Sandy closed her sermon by saying, the prodigal son, when he came to his senses, realized that where he was at, he did not belong in such a mess when he had a good home to go to and said, 'I'm going back to my father'. *Parents. Our children go through a state of mind thinking, I'm grown. I can do what I want'. Then they realize, 'I can't make it out here on my own'. And hopefully they return home. Like the mother of the prodigal son, when things got out of place, she didn't give up and neither should you. Call on the Lord. There is always an answer and a way out. Learn to look to the Lord for help."* **"I will lift up mine eyes unto the hills from whence cometh my help. My help cometh from the Lord Psalm 121:1 KJV.**

Dana said, "I loved what happened when Pastor Sandy was done with her sermon. So many people, including the children, stood up and clapped for her. Also, Steph, like David, when he came to his senses, in that abandoned building, he realized that was not where he belonged. He was glad that the police found the three of them. 'I'm going back home. I messed up.' When he first ran away, he probably thought they would be all right. Like the prodigal son, it didn't turn out that way. Isn't that something how Pastor Sandy's sermon and Daniel's family situation is similar? I really enjoyed church today," Dana said as she started to curl up on the couch in her fuzzy white blanket. As Dana was falling asleep, she said, "Like Aunt Trudy would say, 'It was an In and Out Service.' For me, so much is staying in me from that sermon."

What do you do when things get out of order? Lean not to your own understanding; you are not smart enough to put things back in place. **Lamentations 3:22-23 KJV "It is of the LORD's mercies that we are not consumed, Because his compassions fail not. They are new every morning: Great is thy faithfulness."** *In other words, the Lord's love never ends. His mercies never stop. They are new every morning. Lord, your loyalty is great.*

But those who wait on the Lord shall renew their strength; They shall mount up with wings like eagles, They shall run and not be weary, They shall walk and not faint" Isaiah 40:31 NKJV

"Casting all your care upon Him, for He cares for you"
I Peter 5:6-7 NKJV

In your life, there are going to be times when things are out of place. What do you do? Remember this: *"Have I not commanded you? Be strong and of good courage; do not be afraid, nor be dismayed, for the Lord your God is with you wherever you go" Joshua 1:9 NKJV*.

"Then David danced before the Lord with all his might"
2 Samuel 6:14 NKJV

So, I Danced!

CHAPTER 6
Standing On The Promises

"For I know the plans I have for you, declares the Lord, plans to prosper you and not to harm you, plans to give you hope and a future"
Jeremiah 29:11 NIV

As Dana and Stephanie were saying goodbye to their Aunt Trudy, Dana said, "Can you believe that Aunt Trudy came to church, not one or two but three Sundays in a row? That's record-breaking for her. Go Aunt Trudy." Suddenly, Dana stopped walking and said, "Hey Steph, isn't that Chad over there sitting in that car?"

"I think so. It looks like him but that guy has short hair and Chad wears his hair in locks. He's worn them for years," Stephanie said. "It's been a while since we've seen him. What a year or more?"

Before they could say anything else, the guy got out of his car and walked towards them. "That's Chad all right," Dana said. "But what is wrong with him? He looks, well, different. Not smiling like he usually is. Kinda sad looking."

"Hey ladies, how are you doing?" Chad said as he walked towards them. He tried to put on a smile. "I was wondering if you two have plans this afternoon. I want to take you out to lunch or early dinner. I really could talk to somebody right now. But if you have plans, maybe tomorrow or another day. I'll understand."

Stephanie and Dana said, almost in unison, "No, we were going home."

"You two have not changed—typical twins. Still saying the same thing at the same time," Chad said with a chuckle. "Would you like to go to Oscar Seafood? We don't have to have reservations."

Again, Stephanie and Dana said, almost in unison, "Sure. Sounds great." They looked at each other and laughed.

At lunch before their food was delivered, Chad couldn't stop talking. He told Stephanie and Dana that he really appreciated their taking the time with him. He said that he didn't want to bother his wife too much; she has a lot on her plate with her mother's sickness and all. I mentioned to her that I would talk to you after church if you were available. Then

Chad stops talking for a few seconds, puts his head down a little, and says, "It is about my job. First of all, I have been working like crazy for the past six years at the Rally's Newsline as a journalist."

Chad then shared numerous things. He said the head producer had promised him a promotion about four or five times over the last three years if he did an "outstanding job" on specific projects and the producer said, "I did outstanding work." Chad also said that journalists hired after him were promoted within less than 2 years, except for 2 of them. So, when he mentioned something to the producer about getting promoted, he told me, "I promise you, Chad, your time is coming."

"Promises, promises. That's all I keep getting from him," Chad said. "It's so frustrating. And I'm not going to lie, it really hurts. I'm so disappointed with the producer." *Have you ever been promised something, only for the promise to keep falling through? I know I have. So, what do you do?*

Stephanie said, "Chad, you were in church today, right? Did you listen to what the Pastor said in his sermon? He talked about the promises of God."

Dana chimed in, "One thing about God's promises, Pastor said repeatedly throughout his sermon, He keeps them. People are known for breaking promises. God never does. He never lies, and He never fails. The song that we sang before his sermon, "Standing on the promises of God" is so true. Think about the words of the song."

"Standing on the promises of Christ, my King, Through eternal ages let His praises ring; "Glory in the highest," I will shout and sing, standing on the promises of God. Standing, standing, standing on the promises of God my Savior; Standing, standing, I'm standing on the promises of God."

Stephanie said, "Chad, it's a fact that when you stand on the promises of Christ, in my opinion, it means to rely on those promises when we are faced with challenges, regardless of how hard they are. The song is telling us, as you listen to all the lyrics, that we should trust Jesus as he will guide us as we follow and stand with Him."

Chad said, "I understand what you are saying, and it sounds so easy. But when you are in the midst of things and feel undervalued, not appreciated, never given credit and receiving broken promises repeatedly, it can get to you and be a bit frustrating. Ladies, after a while, I'm not going to lie, it hurts. As a husband, a dad and the main provider, I want to give my family more. I want to trust and believe God will help me and work things out, but right now, I doubt that He understands the pain and suffering that I am going through. I hadn't been to church in such a long time, but this morning I felt the urge to come. Not only to talk to you two, but there was this urgency in me. My mother-in-law is deathly sick. My wife is overwhelmed. At times, I think the children don't know what to say or do when they hear my wife and me whispering, and occasionally she cries. Sometimes, I do trust and believe in God. I really do. And that He can do the impossible, so I've read in the Bible and have been told, but right now, all that I am going through, ladies, it's tough. I mean hard." Chad was so overwhelmed that he kept looking down and shaking his head as he talked.

What are promises? To sum it up in my words: A promise is a declaration that something will or will not happen, often with conditions attached. I read that promises are usually specific and come with conditions. For example, God promises in His word, in the Old and New Testaments, that He will never leave us.

"Be strong and courageous. Do not be afraid or terrified because of them, for the Lord your God goes with you; he will never leave you nor forsake you" Deuteronomy 31:6 NIV

"Keep your lives free from the love of money and be content with what you have, because God has said, 'Never will I leave you; never will I forsake you'" Hebrews 13:5 NIV

When I was a Girl Scout Leader back in the day, I remember teaching the Scouts and holding them to their promise. I'm not even sure if the promise is still taught, used or even practiced today. The promise states, "On my honor, I will try to serve God and my country, to help people at all times, and to live by the Girl Scout Law." The purpose of the Girl Scout Promise was to define how Girl Scouts agreed to act every day toward people in the world and toward one another.

Stephanie put her hand on top of Chad's right hand and said, " I don't want to sound preachy and all that, but God is a promise keeper. Chad you just said that you trust and believe in the Lord and that He can and will do the impossible. Well stand on His promises. I used to hear a verse quoted so much from the senior Saints in the church when they were struggling. I looked it up and I needed to really understand if it was true and found out that it is.

"I was young and now I am old, yet I have never seen the righteous

forsaken or their children begging bread" Psalms 37:25 NIV

Dana said, "Steph, I love the Children's version that says: **'I was young, and now I am old. But I have never seen the Lord leave good people helpless. I have never seen their children begging for food'"** Psalms 37:25 ICB.

Stephanie said, "I agree with Dana, I love the Children's version also. What about you Chad do you believe that? Especially the part where it says, "*I have never seen the Lord leave good people helpless."* You're a good person Chad. Even though the producer made "air" promises, remember that God makes promises that you can rely on. He took care of you before and He will do it again. I know it seems rough right now, overwhelming even. You are frustrated. Sometimes God doesn't give us what we want when we think we should have it. He may have something better in store for us. That's why we must trust Him."

Stephanie also said, "Chad, **Philippians 4:19 KJV** is a verse that should encourage your heart: **'But my God shall supply all your need according to his riches in glory by Christ Jesus.'** Another way of saying it: "**And my God will liberally supply (fill until full) your every need according to His riches in glory in Christ Jesus"** Philippians 4:19 AMP.

"Do you believe that?" Dana said. "These are promises from God's Word in the Bible. You are looking at the promotion that the producer didn't give you. He is judging you on your work but try to concentrate on what God is doing for you. There is a scripture that literally says, Chad if you can believe it, that **'God is the judge and promotions don't come from man'**. Promotions come from God. I know that it is hard to believe at times, but it is true. God promotes us.

"For promotion cometh neither from the east, nor from the west, Nor from the south. But God is the judge: He putteth down one, and setteth up another" Psalm 75:6-7 KJV. When we are overwhelmed, like you are right now, we may feel like God has forgotten about us but that is far from the truth."

"Chad," Dana said, "I want you to do something. Visualize yourself relaxing, sitting on the beach, looking out at the ocean and the wind is softly blowing sand around. The only sound that you hear is the ocean waves hitting against the rocks. You close your eyes for a few seconds. Imagine opening your eyes and you are sitting right next to God. He smiles at you. From your heart, what would you say to Him? What would you ask Him?"

Chad looked at Dana and said, "First of all, I can't even imagine sitting next to God. Second, after my heart stopped racing like a motorboat out of control, I would, I guess, Dana, I don't know. I mean God sitting next to me. Wow, that's special." As Chad was talking, his eyes widened. "Me and God, sitting on the beach talking. After the initial shock wears off, I believe I would tell Him everything. I would tell Him about my family, the sufferings, being overwhelmed and yep, I would tell Him about all the broken promises that were made to me not just from the producer but in life. I would tell Him that I feel like I am at a breaking point and I don't know what to do."

As their food arrives, the waitress asks, "Is everything okay?"

Chad thought she was talking to him because tears were flowing down his cheeks and hitting the table. He said, "I'm going to be all right. I have a lot on my mind."

The waitress said, "I was talking about the food."

The three of them chuckled, and Stephanie said, "Everything looks great. Thank you."

Can you for one second imagine God sitting next to you on a beach? Close your eyes. Inhale. Exhale. As you exhale, slowly open your eyes and turn to your right. There He is. God is sitting next to you. First of all, how will you know that it is God? Trust me, you will know His presence. He calls you by your name and says, "How are you doing?" Can you even imagine your response? Would you try to tell Him what you think He wants to hear or like me just start babbling nonstop and let the tears of joy flow? This is God not only talking to you but sitting right next to you. Sitting next to God so why not give Him all your concerns and worries? Don't hold back. If necessary, let the tears of pain, hurt, suffering, rejection and disappointment run down your face. Let your runny nose run; don't try to dab at it. Give God your honest feelings. Lay down any and every burden. Then after all the ugly crying, a little hollering from what you are going through and have been through, give Him your praise of thanksgiving. Praise Him for forgiveness. Praise Him for never leaving you alone. Just start praising Him like you have lost your mind. **Matthew 11:28 NKJV "Come to Me, all you who labor and are heavy laden, and I will give you rest.** *Sitting next to God. Wow. Right? Hallelujah!!* **God is literally with us each and every day. Don't ever** *forget that.*

Dana looked directly at Chad and said, "Take this setback or not getting the promotion that you feel that you deserve and make it a stepping-stone lesson for yourself and possibly a teaching tool. Did you ever think that just maybe God is trying to tell you something? You feel that you deserve more, but 'more' is not necessary from the job that you are presently in. It is a possibility that you need to step out on faith, trust God and apply for something else, even if it is at another news network."

Chad said, "Oh my goodness. That is so strange you would say that. For the past two or three weeks I've seen this job advertised and I ignored it. I was trying to hold off until I heard something from the producer. I know that must be God speaking through you. I even said something to my wife indirectly. She said, "It won't hurt to apply. What's the worst that can happen?" You are right. Reminds me of that scripture. Ask and you'll get it. Then those doors are gonna open up. Something like that." All three of them chuckled.

"Ask, and it shall be given you; seek, and ye shall find; knock, and it shall be opened unto you: for every one that asketh receiveth; and he that seeketh findeth; and to him that knocketh it shall be opened"
Matthew 7:7-8 KJV

Stephanie said, "Look at Chad quoting the scriptures. All right, Mr. Preacher. But did you get the message? Just maybe the lesson for you is to trust God. We talked about it earlier. Things may seem difficult and out of control but even in your most difficult situations, God is still in control. The Lord is good, and He will always keep His promises to His people."

Have you ever been in a situation where you knew you needed to make a change? You kept holding onto something that just maybe God was trying to tell you to let go of. He had something bigger and better for you. I know for a fact that I have and once I was obedient, God blessed me. The first time I retired, God had been speaking to me to leave. I wanted a certain number of years before retiring. On the job, things were getting worse and complicated. I was crying on the way to work and on the way home. The treatment of certain people, unbelievable and unbearable. I was determined to hold on to a job that was killing me. My health was failing me. The job was full of stress, stress and more stress. God had other plans. He had other opportunities for me. I couldn't see it until after I retired. Once I said yes. I stepped out on faith and retired. What a blessing. What peace. What about you? Are you holding onto something that God told you to let go? Thinking that if I hold out, things will change. It's evaluation time. Trust God. Walk by faith. Then, it's time to stand on the promises of God. Let it go.

As they were getting ready to leave the restaurant, Dana said, "Chad God has a plan for your future. You must trust and believe that He will be there and work things out. I'm sure it is overwhelming right now but consider what we have talked about. Believe God's Word. Trust His Word. Then walk by faith and not by sight. Those words are in the Bible. God is not a person who will lie to you. Can you believe that? Even though the producer made numerous promises and did not keep them, that is not God. When God makes a promise, He keeps it.

> **"The Lord is not slack concerning His promise, as some count slackness, but is longsuffering toward us, not willing that any should perish but that all should come to repentance" II Peter 3:9 NKJV**

Stephanie said, "Before we leave, let's pray believing and trusting God for your change, new beginning and the opening of doors that will be a blessing not only for you but for your entire family." Stephanie prayed quietly. When she said amen, she heard a few other voices chiming in, Amen. A gentleman at the table behind them said, "My family and I could hear from time to time your conversation. We were totally encouraged. What you were talking about is something like what we are going through right now. So, I know this was God-ordained. These tears that you see are tears of joy. Thank you."

Stephanie said, "Of course. God always has a purpose, a plan as to where we should be and what we should hear. May the Lord continue to bless you and your family."

Dana said, "See Chad not only did you get some answers, but the other family, they were blessed also."

"You two, thank you so much. I need to get going; my wife and the children will be back home later this evening and I need to fix a few things up before they arrive. I appreciate you," Chad said as they walked out of the restaurant.

"And we appreciate you for even considering talking to us about your situation. It's going to be all right but you must take the first step for things to start changing. Trust God things are going to work out," Dana said as she got into the car.

"Faith is taking the first step even when you don't see the whole staircase" Dr. Martin Luther King

Can you relate to Chad's story? Have you ever felt like or been in a similar situation? If so, it is nothing to be ashamed of. Promises have been made to each and every one of us. Some promises are fulfilled while others are broken but the promises of God you can rely on.

As you are reading this, have you ever really thought about the promises of God in the Bible? Or, were you one of those persons who feel that the Bible is just made up of numerous stories? Perhaps you are one of those people who think God fulfilled all His promises in the Bible right away. Not so. There are countless stories of when God made His people wait for what He had promised. A few of them that stand out personally for me, as a child, going to Vacation Bible School, was Jonah waiting in the belly of a whale. Can you believe this man was in a whale? The Bible says, **"Now the LORD had prepared a great fish to swallow up Jonah. And Jonah was in the belly of the fish three days and three nights" Jonah 1:17 KJV.**

Abraham waited 25 years for God to give Him a promised son. Who waits 25 years for a son? Some people would have given up after a year or two but the Bible says, **"And the LORD visited Sarah as he had said, and the LORD did unto Sarah as he had spoken. For Sarah conceived, and bare Abraham a son in his old age, at the set time of which God had spoken to him" Genesis 21:1-2 KJV.**

Mary and Martha waited for Jesus, who came 4 days after their brother had died. So, they waited on Jesus; they just knew He would come before their brother died. God had something else planned. The Bible says, **"Then when Jesus came, he found that he had lain in the grave four days already." John 11:17 KJV.** The plan is to see the glory of God. The Bible says, **"Jesus said to her, 'Did I not say to you that if you would believe you would see the glory of God?' And he who had died came out bound hand and foot with graveclothes, and his face was wrapped with a cloth. Jesus said to them, 'Loose him, and let him go'" John 11:40, 44 NKJV.**

Sometimes we must wait on God. While waiting, remember that God is always fighting for you. If He promised it, it will happen. Have you ever seen professional fighters on television in a boxing ring? The two fighters (opponents) are supposed to fight for 10 rounds. Sometimes the boxing match only makes it to round five or six because one of the fighters was not able to withstand the punches and their trainer threw in *the white towel. The white towel symbolizes that it is enough – to quit in defeat and stop the fight. The fighter is taking too much punishment and not able to defend themselves. I'm familiar with the "white towel" phase because when I was growing up, I enjoyed watching the different boxing matches and occasionally I would see the white towel thrown in.*

Do you want to know something? God never uses a "white towel" for He will never be defeated. God wins all His battles. God never loses or fails. Again, God is always fighting for you. Also did you ever think that God cares about little ole you and He made promises to you? Yes, God cares about you and yes, all those promises in the Bible, they are for you. Isn't that something? So, I guess now you are going to ask me what promises God has made to me? I'm glad you asked. Here are several:

God's Love: **"For God so loved the world, that he gave his only Son, that whoever believes in him should not perish but have eternal life" John 3:16 NKJV**

Forgiveness of Sins: **"If we confess our sins, he is faithful and just to forgive us our sins and to cleanse us from all unrighteousness" 1 John 1:9 NKJV**

Strength and Guidance: **"I will instruct you and teach you in the way you should go; I will counsel you with my eye upon you" Psalm 32:8 NKJV**

Provision for Needs: **"And my God will supply every need of yours according to his riches in glory in Christ Jesus" Philippians 4:19 NKJV**

Protection: **"He who dwells in the shelter of the Most High will abide in the shadow of the Almighty. I will say to the Lord, My refuge and my fortress, my God, in whom I trust" Psalm 91:1-2 NKJV**

Peace: **"Peace I leave with you; my peace I give you. I do not give to you as the world gives. Do not let your hearts be troubled and do not be afraid" John 14:27 NKJV**

Comfort: **"Blessed be the God and Father of our Lord Jesus Christ, the Father of mercies and God of all comfort, who comforts us in all our affliction, so that we may be able to comfort those who are in any affliction, with the comfort with which we ourselves are comforted by God" 2 Corinthians 1:3-4 NKJV**

Eternal Life: **"For the wages of sin is death, but the free gift of God is eternal life in Christ Jesus our Lord" Romans 6:23 NKJV**

Answered Prayer: **"If you abide in me, and my words abide in you, ask whatever you wish, and it will be done for you" John 15:7 NKJV**

Victory over Death: **"O death, where is your victory? O death, where is your sting" 1 Corinthians 15:55 NKJV**

Homework and Challenge Time:

1. ***Homework***: Go through the Bible and see if you can list some of the other promises that God has made to you. Always remember that God is not only a promise-maker but also a promise-keeper. Do you believe God keeps his promises? Why or why not?

2. ***Challenge***: Just for one day consider writing down every time you make a promise to someone. See if you can keep them. Just one day. Promises such as: I will call you in a minute. I will have that stuff ready by this afternoon. I will fix that table. Don't worry about it, I will take care of things. I will be home shortly. I will be right back, etc. At the end of the day, look at your list. Did you fulfill every one of those promises? Was it easy? I'm sure it wasn't. We all make promises and sometimes we don't keep them. Again, remember that God is a promise-maker and keeper.

So here we go. In order for you to dance like David danced, remember my "He wills." No matter what, the Lord has promised that He will fight for you. He will never leave you. He will make a way for you. He will always protect you. He will provide for you. He will not lie. He will be faithful. And most of all <u>He will always love</u>.

For I know the plans I have for you, declares the Lord, plans to prosper you and not to harm you, plans to give you hope and a future" Jeremiah 29:11, NIV

"Then David danced before the Lord with all his might"
2 Samuel 6:14 NKJV

So, I Danced!

Chapter 7
Why The Tambourine Mariam

"Then Aaron's sister Miriam, who was a prophetess, took a tambourine in her hand. All the women followed her, playing tambourines and dancing" Exodus 15:20 ICB

Mandi ran into the choir room and said aloud, "I want to play the tambourine and dance like Miriam danced in the Bible. She danced because of what God had done for the Israelites and how He saved them by getting them through the Red Sea on dry land and when she had to leave her homeland abruptly, she could only take a few things. Sister girl took her tambourine with her. Somebody give me a tambourine! I want to give God praise."

Garry the choir director and Dana were sitting in the corner talking when he said, "Mandi, do share why all the excitement. Let us rejoice with you." Mandi, trying to catch her breath said, "Well, remember last week when the bad storm came through and certain sections of the city got flooded. Many streets were flooded, and thousands also lost power. So many people were misplaced. Some people lost everything they owned. Well for those of you that didn't know it, I live in that flooded area." Before she finished saying what she was going to say, she was cut off.

Ted said quickly, "Oh Mandi, we are so sorry. We didn't know. I missed seeing you last week and at church this week, but I thought you were working. What can we do to help you?"

Dana added in a high-pitched voice, "Mandi, oh my goodness. I am so sorry. I agree with Ted. What can we do to help you? Lord have mercy on Mandi."

Different choir members started chiming in until finally Mandi said, "There is nothing anyone can do to help me."

Garry said, "Mandi there is nothing to be ashamed about if you need help. We can all pitch in. Right?" As he looked around the room everyone was in total agreement. "And you know for a fact we will stick right by you until you are up on your feet. That's what we do here. You witnessed firsthand when Deb and her family went through something similar to what you are going through last year. We were all there. Supporting her."

Dana said, "If my memory serves me correctly, you were the first person to step up to help organize things. And you stuck by her after everything was done. We will do the same for you, Mandi."

Deb, who had quietly slipped into rehearsal, said, "Mandi, my family and I will forever be grateful for all that you did for us, and Dana is right, plus all that you continue to do. So, what do you need or want us to do for you? How can we all help?"

Before Mandi knew what was happening, the entire choir had surrounded her. She could hear voices in the crowd say things like, "We're here for you. You're not by yourself. Everything is going to be all right. Let us help."

Mandi said, "Everyone, I am so touched by the outpouring of love and support. I thank God that I am involved in a choir that not only sings about love but shows it all the time. When I moved here from Ohio, I had no family. You all welcomed me and became my extended family. So, thank you."

Before Mandi could finish speaking again, she heard in the crowd, "You are family and, that's what families do. Look out for each other. Take care of one another". And someone added, "Yes, that's right. We got you Mandi."

So, Mandi shouted, "Hold it, everyone. Yes, I am in the flooded area. But remember I said when I was coming in that "I feel like playing the tambourine and dancing like Miriam danced in the Bible. She danced because of what God had done. Well, I want to dance because all that God has done for me."

Dana said quickly, "What do you mean, Mandi?"

"Well, when the city finally gave the residents permission to go back into our homes, I just knew that everything was going to be wet and muddy because of how high the water level was. I mean, it was scary high to the tops of some buildings and low to first-floor dwellings. I could hear different people saying as they opened their door to their apartment where I live, "Oh my goodness, this is a mess. I heard someone else say I think I lost everything." Mandi paused for a few seconds.

"Yes, I was scared to death to open my door. I prayed first and asked God to give me the strength to handle whatever is on the other side of the door." Mandi took a few deep breaths as tears flowed down her cheeks. Dana put her hand in Mandi's hand for support as she was talking. Someone gave her a tissue.

Then Mandi said, "But praise be to God. When I opened the door, I couldn't believe it. It was dry. I walked around, holding my breath, looking to see areas with mud or water lingering. Nope. The only water that got into my apartment was in the bathroom. Not my bedrooms, the kitchen, the living room nor the closets. Just a little water on the floor in the bathroom and that was because I had the window slightly cracked. So, I scrubbed and bleached the bathroom floor. Then, to be on the safe side, I cleaned the rest of my apartment. I changed all the bedding and did the laundry. I threw out the garbage and a little bit of stuff on the counters. Done. Cleaned as if there had never been a storm. I was also able to help my two neighbors. Things weren't as bad as they thought once we all pitched in to help each other. We helped each other by throwing things out, scrubbing things down, doing the laundry and food shopping. So as of today, thank you, God, we are literally back in our apartments. That's why when I came in, I said I want to get a tambourine out and dance like Miriam."

Before Mandi could say anything else, the whole choir went up into a spirit of praise and thanksgiving with and for her. You could hear people in the crowd saying, "Praise God. Won't He do it? God is awesome. What a mighty God we serve."

Then the pianist and organist started playing praise music. The drummer lit up the drums and someone started playing the tambourine that was sitting on top of the piano. Suddenly, someone started singing *"God is a good God, yes He is."*

Mandi finally said, "I really do understand why Mariam invited the other women to join in with her in praise and thanksgiving for all that the Lord had done for them. I may not have had a Red Sea experience, but God spared my apartment and, I was able to help my neighbors get settled also. I am so thankful I can share with you all and witness to you what God has done for me. I'm so overwhelmed and grateful at the same time for my miracle."

Dana said, "The Bible says to rejoice with them who rejoice. And we are rejoicing with you."

Rejoice with those who rejoice, and weep with those who weep
Romans 12:15 NKJV

Garry said, "Mandi, the greatest thing you did was to share what God has done for you. Somebody needed to hear your testimony. I truly believe that someone in here was losing faith in what God will do, and you truly encouraged them." Garry stopped talking for a few seconds. He looked around the Choir Room and said, "We have not only heard, but we witnessed through Mandi, what a miracle-working God we serve. So please don't take it for granted when we are singing songs of victory and deliverance. This is a ministry. We minister to the people through songs. So let us pray before we start our rehearsal." The choir said "Amen."

Have you ever experienced something even remotely similar to what Mandi went through? You thought that something was going to turn out horribly and God turned it around. I know that I have. God is so awesome. He is amazing. He is our protector and our provider. He watches over us and takes care of our homes. He knows just what we need. I always whisper a prayer in my home that says, "Bless this house, oh Lord, I pray. Keep it safe both night and day." I grew up hearing that. I vaguely remember it as a song and, without realizing it, I put it somewhere in my heart a long time ago and it has become part of my daily prayer for my home.

After the choir rehearsal, Dana asked Mandi if she needed a ride home. Mandi said yes. This allowed Dana to talk one-on-one with Mandi.

"Mandi," Dana said as she was pulling up in front of Mandi's apartment, "you are always saying that you are a baby in Christ and that you don't know what He wants you to do. You blessed so many of us with your testimony. I agree with Garry, someone was truly encouraged and lifted up. You are always looking for ways to help people. I've watched you give from your own money to help people. So, when you shared what God had done for you, my first thought was Lord, she is so unselfish. Keep asking God what He would have you do. Thank you, Mandi, for all that you do. I pray God's nonstop blessings for you."

"Dana, don't make me cry. Your words are so kind. I'm just doing what I was trained as a child to do which is to help others. Thank you so much for the ride," Mandi said as she got out of the car. "Lord willing, I will see you on Sunday with my *tambourine* in my hand and ready to dance for the Lord for all that He has done for me. I might even act like Miriam on Sunday" she said as she closed the door smiling.

"And let us not grow weary while doing good, for in due season we shall reap if we do not lose heart" Galatians 6:9 NKJV

"Let us not grow weary or become discouraged in doing good, for at the proper time we will reap, if we do not give in" Galatians 6:9 AMP

Who was Miriam and what was Mandi talking about? *As a young girl, I remember reading the story about the Israelites in the Bible. My parents had this great big black Bible with lots of pictures showing some of the events in the Bible. In Exodus (the Old Testament), I got caught up looking at the pictures and not reading all the chapters. So, when I saw the images of Pharaoh's army chasing the Israelites, I would get upset. You see, it says in the Bible that God, through Moses and Aaron, sent word to Pharaoh numerous times to let His people go. Pharaoh would not comply. He was hardheaded and crazy. God sent plagues on the land and after the tenth and final plague, Pharaoh finally sent word to the Israelites in the middle of the night to leave Egypt. So, the Israelites grabbed what they could carry and headed out on foot. They left as quickly as they could before Pharaoh changed his mind.*

The Israelites were some kind of people. They could have been nicer to their leader Moses. I would not have wanted to be Moses. From what I remember, the Israelites were the most complaining people that you would ever want to meet. They complained about any and everything. God instructs the Israelites to camp by the Red Sea. They felt trapped. At one time, they told Moses you should have left us where we were. I know I would have left them. They said we don't want to die when they saw Pharaoh's army coming towards them. I'm sure they gave Moses an earful when they saw the sea in front of them. And they probably said things like, "Are you crazy? Are you trying to drown us?" Still complaining. At one time, from night to morning, things seemed hopeless. Then, they watched as God used Moses to part the Red Sea (lifting his staff) to provide a way for them to safety on dry land through the parted sea. When all the Israelite's were safe and Pharaoh's army was right behind them, they saw that when Moses raised his staff again, the water covered Pharaoh's entire army. They all drowned.

"For the horses of Pharaoh went with his chariots and his horsemen into the sea, and the Lord brought back the waters of the sea upon them. But the children of Israel went on dry land in the midst of the sea"
Exodus 15:19 NKJV

There was a question I always wanted to ask my Sunday School teachers growing up, but I never did: **"What in the world was Miriam doing with a tambourine?"** *Then I understood later, the more that I read and studied the Bible. Again, the Israelites only had time to grab a few necessary items* and leave. A tambourine, you would have thought would have been pretty low on the list of priorities of things to take with you. Miriam, though, packed her tambourine. She probably sensed that a time would come when she would use it. She didn't know where Moses was taking them to or how things would turn out but Miriam being a prophetess, was counting on God to deliver them and to protect them. She had faith and believed that God would deliver them from the hands of the enemy (Pharaoh). She was right and God did just that. Miriam trusted her gut instinct; she took her tambourine when she was fleeing. She was going to get her praise on.

The Israelites, when they saw what happened to the Egyptians that were pursuing them (all of them drowned), stood on the bank and praised God. They sang and danced. Then Miriam pulled out a tambourine and began to lead the women in singing, dancing and praising the Lord for what He had done for them.

> **"Then Miriam the prophetess, the sister of Aaron, took the timbrel in her hand; and all the women went out after her with timbrels and with dances. And Miriam answered them: 'Sing to the Lord, For He has triumphed gloriously! The horse and its rider He has thrown into the sea'" Exodus 15:20-21 NKJV**

Pharaoh's army which was chasing and trying to pursue the Israelites, meant nothing but to harm them. God had another plan. The same thing He has for your life when people set up all kinds of traps for you and try and come at you in different ways. They try their best to hurt you. You know I'm telling the truth. But God has a plan. So, let the tears fall. Let disappointment happen. Have a pity party and temporarily isolate yourself **BUT** then, get up. Get your tambourine out. Put your dancing shoes on. Then, dance and praise God like you have lost your mind.

Don't dance and play the tambourine alone; do like Mariam did—invite others to dance with you. For those who don't know, I am a tambourine player. I don't just play when I hear other musical instruments or when the choir is singing. The tambourine has become a time of deliverance for me— a time of healing, a time of being set free.

> **"Praise Him with the timbrel and dance; Praise Him with stringed instruments and flutes! Praise Him with loud cymbals; Praise Him with clashing cymbals" Psalms 150:4-5 NKJV**

I'm finally home," Dana said to Stephanie as she fell into the house and plopped on the couch, kicking her shoes off. "Stephie, you are not going to believe what happened in Choir Rehearsal today. To God be the glory."

"Now to Him who is able to do exceedingly abundantly above all that we ask or think, according to the power that works in us, to Him be glory in the church by Christ Jesus to all generations, forever and ever. Amen"
Ephesians 3:20-21 NKJV

"Then David danced before the Lord with all his might"
2 Samuel 6:14 NKJV

So, I Danced!

Chapter 8
I Feel A Change Coming

"You will keep him in perfect peace, whose mind is stayed on You because he trusts in you" Isaiah 26:3 NKJV

Have you ever felt a change coming before it happened? Or have you ever been led to do something and you didn't know where it was coming from? I am sure in your lifetime that you were led to do something that felt odd, and you did it anyway even though it didn't make sense only later to realize you were glad you went with your gut instinct. It was a change from the norm or the opposite. You wish you had done what your gut was telling you to do because if you had, you wouldn't have a particular problem or be in an odd situation. Or do you like things to stay the way they are—no changing them? Always keep in mind that sometimes change is good. Change is necessary. I have been on both sides. I listened and acted, and, then there was the time I should have listened and acted.

*When God tells you to do something, just do it. Don't question Him. Don't be disobedient. Don't have the "it doesn't make sense attitude." He will never ask you to do something contradictory to scripture and will never ask you to sin or do something Jesus Christ wouldn't do. Be willing to change. God **knows** what the best is. He **wants** what is best for you. **Trust Him**. Again, change is good. Change is necessary. The question is are you ready for the change?*

"Trust in the Lord with all your heart and lean not on your own understanding; In all your ways acknowledge Him, And He shall direct your paths" Proverbs 3:5-6 NKJV

"Trust the Lord with all your heart. Don't depend on your own understanding. Remember the Lord in everything you do. And he will give you success" Proverbs 3:5-6 ICB

*I remember a song called **"Changed"** by Tramaine Hawkins that we used to sing in church. It was one of those songs that literally made you think about yourself.*

A change, a change has come over me
He changed my life and now I'm free
He washed away all my sins and He made me whole
He washed me white as snow (snow)
He changed
My life complete
And now I sit
I sit at His feet
To do
What must be done
I'll work and work
Until He comes
A wonderful change (a wonderful, a wonderful change)
Has come over me (has come over me)
A wonderful change (wonderful change)
Has come over me

There are many other lyrics to this song, but the main statement is saying a change has come over me (you). Everyone should want a change in life. For change is good. Change is necessary.

Change was something that Stephanie not only needed but also wanted. She could not wait to get to her next session, so she left work an extra hour early. Not just to get to her session, but to start doing things a little differently. She wanted to walk around the college campus near Mrs. Emma's (her therapist's) office. She was glad to find a parking spot not only near the campus but also close to her appointment. After walking around and admiring the beautiful buildings on campus for about 20 minutes, Stephanie sat down on a bench about 3 minutes away. Sitting there, she started thinking about what got her to the point of needing help and, literally thanking Dana, her twin sister and best friend, for noticing a negative change in her.

Has anyone ever told you that you were acting negatively? And, if they did, how did you feel? Be honest. For me, I felt offended. But in reality, they were right. I had to make some changes. Later I was glad I did make those changes. It helped me to grow and become a better person.

"I cannot believe that I have been seeing Mrs. Emma for five months already," Stephanie said to herself.

As she sat, she watched college students laughing and hollering playfully as they tossed a Frisbee. "Looks like they are having so much fun" she whispered to herself. She could also faintly hear singing. Then she noticed a small group of people either practicing or just singing while sitting under a large weeping willow tree. The harmony was out of this world.

Laughter. Running. Playing. Singing. Talking. These are the things that Stephanie noticed people were doing while she was sitting on the bench. As she sat, she could feel the cool Fall breeze blowing her hair and the afternoon sunshine as it beamed down on her face. Stephanie thought, "What a perfect day to be sitting outside."

Then for some unknown reason, she clapped her hands twice with excitement. She started thinking about her change in attitude, accountability and action over the past five months. Triple A's as Mrs. Emma calls them. "I've come a mighty long way" she said as she got up from the bench and started walking towards her therapist's office. "Yep, I sure have."

She couldn't wait to share with Mrs. Emma some of the discussions that she and Dana had been having with so many different people. They would come to them for help and suggestions, but in reality, Dana and Stephanie were the ones being helped. One day out of the blue Dana said to Stephanie, "I feel so much better after talking and taking the time out to help people." Stephanie said, "You were saying what I have been thinking for the longest time." *What about you? Have you ever felt like that? Someone came to you for help, and you felt better after helping them. I know I do all the time.*

When Stephanie arrived at the building, she decided to take the stairs instead of the elevator to Mrs. Emma's Office. As she entered the office, she stopped for a few seconds. The receptionist looked at her and said, "Stephanie, are you all right? Do you need to sit down?"

Stephanie held up one finger to signal she was fine. Then she said softly, "I ran up the stairs instead of taking the elevator. I don't know why I did that. I thought it would be easy. Silly me." Then the two of them chuckled.

Don't tell me I'm the only one who has done that. Thinking, I could run up the stairs and not take the elevator. Why? Then halfway up the stairs regretting it. Yep. I've done that numerous times. What about you? Have you done that too? Be honest.

Before Stephanie could sit down and catch her breath, Mrs. Emma opened her office door and welcomed Stephanie in. "How are you doing today,

Steph? I love that yellow on you. Your dress is so pretty" Mrs. Emma said as Stephanie sat down in the big black leather chair.

"I'm doing really well. Before I came today, I did something different. I went for a walk on the college campus and then I sat outside on a bench for a while. I really enjoyed sitting and watching people. You learn so much by just watching them," Stephanie said. "And how are you doing today?"

Mrs. Emma said, "I'm doing well too. Thank you for asking. I need to take time and sit outside too. It is so refreshing." As she adjusted her laptop on the desk, she asked, "How have you been since your last appointment?"

"I feel like I am finally making progress especially since I am focusing on my Triple A's: attitude, accountability and actions. It's a little bit harder than I thought but an eye opener for me" Stephanie said.

"How so?" Mrs. Emma asked.

Stephanie said, "For instance, <u>before</u> my sessions on dealing with my Triple A's, if someone would say to me, 'Seems like you have an attitude problem,' and I didn't because I was just being quiet, I would literally get an attitude because they mentioned it. Now I realize that I am not responsible for how or what people think or feel about me. But, accountability-wise, I will admit if I have an attitude. If I do, action-wise, I will deal with it right away. What is causing this attitude? How do I handle it? How do I change? Then do what is necessary to get rid of it." *(The above came from Genia Moten's solutions to life problems called* ***"What She Would Do"*** *book that has not been published yet)*.

"If you can't change it, change your attitude" Maya Angelou

"Not everything that is faced can be changed. But nothing can be changed until it is faced" James Baldwin

Mrs. Emma said, "Stephanie, you are making great progress. What are your thoughts on that?"

Stephanie looked out the window before answering Mrs. Emma. She noticed a two-tone grayish sparrow walking on the windowsill. Then she said, "My change is coming about because I have literally been seeking God for directions and answers." Stephanie paused then she continued,

"When I first started looking at me I literally did not like what I saw. Dana pointed out some of the things that I am seeing now but I was in denial. Now, I am beginning to feel confident and good about myself. Some of the changing steps were painful. Again, I couldn't believe it was me. The more honest I was with myself, the better I felt. Change is good and necessary."

There are all kinds of changes, from personality to attitude. Physical. So, stop now. Take a good look at yourself in the mirror. Suppose you looked in the mirror and your outfit did not look the way you thought it would? What do you do? Change it, right?

To move forward, start by being honest. So, what do you want to change to be a better person? Seriously. Your hair color (*I might try that*), your makeup (*I'm not a big makeup person*), or possibly a nose job (*I like mine*). Maybe lose weight, gain weight or consider a total wardrobe change. Change is good. Sometimes, change is necessary.

As you read earlier, Stephanie recognizes that she had to make some changes. She had to make some attitude adjustments. Her accountability had to be in check. She needed to be mindful of her actions. If the truth be told, we all have work to do on ourselves. We can all make changes to our attitudes or to our character. No one is perfect. We are all striving for perfection.

Go ahead and take the leap. You want to be a better person? Make the necessary changes. I dare you to ask the Lord to turn the searchlight on your heart and take away anything that ought not to be. Sit still. Be quiet. Inhale. Exhale. Count backwards 6-5-4-3-2-1. Close your eyes for 30 seconds. Let Him show you. When He shows you what needs to be changed, be prepared for the change to start.

"Be still, and know that I am God; I will be exalted among the nations, I will be exalted in the earth" Psalms 46:10 NKJV

Stephanie took over five months to start feeling and seeing the major changes in her life. What about you? Are you ready? The change won't happen overnight—one step at a time. There might be some "ouch" moments, the I can't believe that I'm like that glimpse or the, no, no way, that is me in the mirror, I don't like what I see.

Change happens one step, two steps, then three steps at a time. Before you know it, yeah, you are walking towards change. Are you ready?

Remember I said, we are not perfect. We are striving for perfection.

Do you feel any changes starting to come about as you are reading this? Mentally. In your heart. Yes. No. I dare you to look in the mirror again. This time, smile at yourself and say, "Today I will make the first step towards my change." Ask the Lord to **"Guide my steps by your word, so I will not be overcome by evil" Psalms 119:133 NLT.** *Then day by day watch a change come about.*

Keep this in mind. Yes, change is good and necessary in this ever-changing world, but one person that never changes and He knows you, that's God. He literally never changes.

> **"For I am the Lord, I do not change" Malachi 3:6a NKJV**

> **"For I am the Lord, I do not change; Therefore you are not consumed, O sons of Jacob" Malachi 3:6 NKJV**

> **"Jesus Christ is the same yesterday, today, and forever" Hebrews 13:8 NKJV**

Mrs. Emma looked at Stephanie and said, "Time went by so quickly today, Steph. I want you to be encouraged. In the past five months, you have made tremendous progress. In our next session, let's talk about completion and rounding things up. What do you say?"

Stephanie smiled and said, "I knew eventually I would be done, but to hear you say it, wow. I do feel the change you were talking about that I would. I know for myself that I have made progress."

As always, Mrs. Emma closed the session with a prayer.

When Stephanie was walking towards the door, she stopped, turned around and asked Mrs. Emma, "Do you ever hug your clients? I could really use one right now."

Mrs. Emma said, "I thought you would never ask." She hugged Stephanie and said, "You should be proud of your progress and accomplishments." Stephanie smiled, then walked out the door towards the steps and not the elevator. "I think I want to walk down the same way I came in. It's easier to go down," she whispered to herself.

Outside, Stephanie almost ran to her car. Once she got in, she said, "I can't wait to tell Dana about my session and what Mrs. Emma said." Then she kept saying, "I feel so much better."

Those words reminded me of a song I used to hear in church.

Glory, Glory, Hallelujah

Glory, glory, hallelujah!
Since I laid my burdens down.
Glory, glory, hallelujah!
Since I laid my burdens down!

Friends don't treat me like they used to
Since I laid my burdens down.
Friends don't treat me like they used to
Since I laid my burdens down!

I'm goin' home to live with Jesus
Since I laid my burdens down.
I'm goin' home to live with Jesus
Since I laid my burdens down!

I feel better, so much better
Since I laid my burdens down.
I feel better, so much better
Since I laid my burdens down!

"Then David danced before the Lord with all his might"
2 Samuel 6:14 NKJV

So, I Danced!

Chapter 9
This Thing Called Rejection. Oh My

"Why are you cast down, O my soul? And why are you disquieted within me? Hope in God; For I shall yet praise Him, the help of my countenance and my God" Psalms 42:11 NKJV

"Blessed is the man who trusts in the Lord and whose hope is the Lord" Jeremiah 17:7 NKJV

Have you ever been around someone, a group of people or even your coworkers and you could tell that they did not want to be bothered by you, or they were upset with you, and you had no idea why? Maybe they are envious of what they think you have. In a crowd or setting, you look towards them only to notice a look of non-approval with the rolling of the eyes or tilting of the head. **Jealousy.**

When you talk, one of two things happens. They cut you off or dismiss what you are saying. They go as far as downplaying the importance of your opinion and ideas as if what you are saying is not valid. **Resentment.**

The final blow is that they exclude you from being made aware of, invited to, and informed about things that are important and what is going on that you should be involved in. When in a crowd, they will talk to everyone but you. Pretend they don't see you as you move forward to speak to them. Suddenly, they get distracted and fail to acknowledge your presence. They make it their business to exclude you from specific conversations. **Rejection.**

Keep in mind that jealousy, resentment, and rejection not only happen to you but also to any leader or a person who is a go-getter, hard worker and/or achiever. Jealousy, resentment and rejection happen to everyone at one time or another. There is always someone or a group of people standing on the sidelines ready to complain, point out and judge what you are doing. But that should not stop you, the leader, or the hard worker from moving forward and doing what you or they are supposed to do.

Dana came into the house, threw her bags down and said aloud, "I thought all this was behind me. What did I do now? Being left out again. God, this hurts."

Dana was not aware that Stephanie was home. She told her that morning she would be working late. "D, what's the matter. What happened?" Stephanie said.

Dana looked up with tears in her eyes and said, "You startled me! I thought you were working late. I thought I was here by myself. Nothing much happened, Steph, except that," Dana paused for a second, then she said, "I'm upset with this lady named Bev in Accounting but she doesn't know it though."

"Talk to me then. Come here, sit down," Stephanie said as she patted the couch. "What do you mean she doesn't know it?"

Dana said, "I was in the corner of the breakroom when Bev walked in with Todd, one of my coworkers to get something out of the refrigerator. They were talking about her housewarming, and yesterday how they, and other coworkers, went to the new restaurant called Sayers. Todd said that, from what he saw at the housewarming, everyone had a wonderful time. He also told Bev she got some great gifts. She agreed. Then he said, "yesterday was out of this world. Who knew everyone was going to cut up at Sayers? That was so much fun." Then, the two of them walked out of the breakroom talking." Dana put her head down. Stephanie reached to hug her and paused.

"Steph," Dana said, "They never noticed me by the cabinet. When they left, I almost fell on the floor gasping for air from what I heard. A housewarming and a new restaurant. How come I was not invited? My head was swirling. I was hurt by what I heard. I've always been there for Bev. When her mother was sick, I prepared meals and ran errands. When her brother passed away, I worked closely with the family and our coworkers to make sure they had food and everything. When her daughter got in trouble, I helped her out, Steph. No one else helped her. I went to the court and the family sessions with her. It was a big secret. I couldn't tell anyone and I still haven't. But yet I'm not good enough to be invited to personal events. I don't get it Steph."

Dana stopped talking for a few seconds, gasping for air as tears flowed down her cheeks, hitting the top of her yellow jacket. Before Stephanie could say anything, Dana said, "I didn't think too much of it until recently, for whatever reason Bev started saying sarcastically, 'Dana, girl you got it made. Everybody likes you and your sister. You two are constantly helping people. If somebody is in trouble, call Dana. Don't know how to solve a family problem, call Dana. Feeling overwhelmed, you had better call Dana and her sister. Who can't you two help? Knowing you two, you probably helped the Mayor when we were having problems in the city. Also, look at you. You always dress nicely. Look nice, act nice and yes lady, smell nice. Every time I see you, you are surrounded by people. You are never alone. Girl, I'm serious, you got it made. No wonder people want to be around you'. Then she would chuckle and walk away."

"Dana, don't you see what that is? *Jealousy.* Bev wants what you have. Indirectly, she is saying that 'I want what you have, Dana. I want to be like you.' She's trying to make a joke out of it, but let's be real, that's straight up jealousy" Stephanie said.

Dana threw a pillow on the floor and said, "And, what is she talking about people always surround me? **Resentment.** On the job, I am always by myself. Trust me, the only time someone is around me is when they have a stupid problem, they need some quick advice, or they need help with something. Steph, it's so unfair. That's crazy, Bev being jealous of me. I'm the one who isn't being invited to parties, housewarmings, weddings, picnics, or to restaurants. *Rejection*. It's so unfair."

Stephanie looked at Dana. She knew the feeling. Instead of saying, that's a shame, I know how you feel Dana. She reminded Dana of how she was there for her. "Remember five not quite six months ago when you suggested that I talk to someone? I got quiet. I couldn't talk to anyone, not even you. I was hurting so bad inside I didn't know what to do. One of the things I couldn't figure out was how I was able to help people, but I wasn't good enough to be invited to their parties, social events or activities. That was a hard pill to swallow for a long time. Going to Mrs. Emma, who's my Christian therapist, she pointed out some good things that helped me. One of the things she did was to make references to people or things in the Bible that were similar or close to what I was going through. Daily she emphasized that I am not responsible for what people think or do towards me. Trust me, it helped. I'm not responsible for people's shortcomings."

Keep in mind when you are reading this: you have no control over people. There is nothing you can do to change how people feel or think about you.

Focus Corner: A, B and C

A. Jealousy
What do you think? Is there ever a time when jealousy is right? Yes. According to the scripture, God is a jealous God. ***"For you shall***

worship no other god, for the Lord, whose name is Jealous, is a jealous God)" Exodus 34:14 NKJV.

God gets jealous when we spend a great deal of time on other things and fail to focus on Him. He is jealous when we spend the majority of our time watching television, reading social media and not reading and studying His Word. He wants us to spend time getting to know Him, just as we do with our friends and loved ones. He wants us to tell Him our problems first instead of calling, telling others and then later talking to Him about our concerns. God is a jealous God for the right reason. He created us. He loves us unconditionally. He wants what is best for us. He wants us to worship Him. Do you think what the scripture says is in vain, *"The Spirit who dwells in us yearns jealously" James 4:5 NKJV.* Do you think this scripture means nothing? *It says, "The Spirit that God made to live in us wants us for himself alone" James 4:5 ICB.*

People are jealous. Let's reverse these two words to say **Are people** jealous of each other? They want what other people have: their family, home, cars, their success, fame, job, and even their beauty. Sometimes they will get so jealous that they cannot control their feelings, actions or emotions towards a person. For you out there, here are a few don'ts: *Don't* become possessive and show insecurity. *Don't* be envious of what someone else has. *Don't* desire what others have. The scripture says: *"You desire but do not have, so you kill. You covet but you cannot get what you want, so you quarrel and fight. You do not have because you do not ask God" James 4:2 NIV.* Hello! Ask God for what you desire and want.

You are jealous. Let's reverse two words. **Are you jealous**? You don't have to be jealous of anyone or what they have. Again, ask God for what you want. Please don't be upset because someone else did the work to achieve their goal. You need to do something to reach yours. Don't keep quiet about how you feel. Unless you say something, that jealousy will eat you up from the inside out if you don't be careful. What is on your heart? What is on your mind? If necessary, confess to someone, "I'm jealous of such and such. Can you pray with me?" That's taking control. That's healing. The Bible says to *"Confess your faults one to another, and pray one for another, that ye may be healed. The effectual fervent prayer of a righteous man availeth much" James 5:16 KJV.* God will give you the desires of your heart. *"Delight yourself also in the Lord, And He shall give you the desires of your heart" Psalms 37:4 NKJV.*

"For where your treasure is, there your heart will be also"
Matthew 6:21 NIV

Let's really be honest. It's just you and me talking. Have you ever been jealous of something someone else had? Vacations they can go on, friends or people they are associated with, jobs that can take care of their needs, their beautiful home or how about their expensive car. Are you jealous to the point you think, why them and why not me? Well? I must confess, at one time or another, yes in my younger years, I was jealous. The key for me to moving forward was to start celebrating and be joyful for them, set goals for myself and make changes. Pray, trust God and, keep in mind, what God has for me, it is for me.

B. From Jealously to Resentment

If one is not careful, jealousy can cause resentment. As I said above, jealousy arises when a person wants what others have, such as their family, homes, cars, their success, fame, job, or even their beauty. Sometimes a person will get so jealous that they cannot control their feelings, actions or emotions towards a person. They may get so jealous that they start resenting the other person. They show bitterness, anger, become frustrated, and outraged for no apparent reason. Not able to focus on what they already have but on what the other person has.

What can one do to stop jealousy from turning into resentment? Again, here are *a few don'ts*: *Don't* keep quiet about how you feel. Apply the scripture above, **"Confess your faults one to another, and pray one for another, that ye may be healed"**. *Don't* compare oneself to others. *Don't* measure one's happiness against another's. *Don't* envy what one thinks another person has (you don't live in their home). **"But as for me, my feet had almost stumbled; My steps had nearly slipped. For I was envious of the boastful, When I saw the prosperity of the wicked" Psalms 73:2-3 NKJV. "But I had almost stopped believing this truth. I had almost lost my faith because I was jealous of proud people. I saw wicked people doing well" Psalms 73:2-3 ICB.**

"Do the best you can until you know better. Then when you know better, do better" Maya Angelo

For jealousy not to turn into resentment, take every one of your problems to the Lord. Believe it when you pray that things will work out. Why? You are encouraged to walk by faith and not by sight. In other words, you can't see it, but you believe it. Know that God loves you for who you are. So, trust the process. You are not alone. God will help you. God will take care of you. (*The above was from the book of Genia Moten that has not been written yet*).

"Fear not, for I am with you; Be not dismayed, for I am your God. I will

strengthen you, Yes, I will help you, I will uphold you with My righteous right hand" Isaiah 41:10 NKJV

C. From Jealously to Resentment to Rejection

There are numerous reasons for something to be rejected and cannot be sold at full price. For instance, an automobile can be rejected by a consumer due to defects or at the time of purchase, the car was not what was described or advertised. In a store, clothes are put in a rejection pile and sold for little to nothing if they have a flaw, such as a snag, a rip in the seams, and/or threads showing where they should not be. Appliances and furniture are placed in the "dent and sold as is" section when they have scratches or are broken.

The above objects are just that, objects. No feelings. No emotions. No concerns. So, it is no big deal if items and things are rejected but the same does not apply to people. ***Jealousy*** can cause resentment. ***Resentment can flow into rejection.*** Something you should know is that some people cannot handle any form of rejection. They are and can be devastated when they are not accepted. Some people will even go as far as suffering in silence due to the loneliness rejection brings to them. Rejection is not prejudice. It hits people of all ages, colors, and nationalities.

I know how it feels to be rejected. I know the feeling of not being accepted. In my younger years, I was rejected so many times that I felt the R in my middle name stood for Rejection, not Rosalie. There were many days I sat alone feeling and bearing the load of rejection. In my young adult years, I was overwhelmed by classmates who did not accept me. Trust me, as I got older, I became wiser. I still cry a little, get upset, and have my fits, but then I taught myself how to limit rejection in a "no parking zone." What does that mean? Don't stay in pain and feel rejection for too long. The Bible says, **"For His anger is but for a moment, His favor is for life; Weeping may endure for a night, But joy comes in the morning" Psalms 30:5 NKJV.**

If you have no idea what it feels like not to be accepted, and you have never been rejected by anyone or any group in your life, then stop reading now. You will not understand. On the other hand, if you are a person who is comfortable rejecting people and not accepting them, this chapter is for you. So, keep reading and maybe you will understand how people are feeling.

There is a person who knows firsthand about ***Jealously, Resentment*** and ***Rejection.*** He walked it, talked it and lived it, but it did not stop Him from completing His assignment on earth. There was a group of people that was *jealous* of who he was, **Resented** Him for what He did and *rejected* Him for what He stood for. That person is Jesus. Yes, Jesus. He was hated by religious leaders of the Jewish people, primarily the Pharisees and Sadducees were jealous of him and his ministry. This jealousy stemmed from several reasons related to power, popularity, and control. Due to Jesus challenging their traditions, teachings, and interpretations of Jewish law, and His claims of divine authority, this opposition eventually led to a plot by these religious leaders to have Him killed. The Gospel of John records them saying, *"If we let him go on like this, everyone will believe in him, and then the Romans will come and take away both our place and our nation" John 11:48 NKJV.* This concern showed their fear of losing control, which was the root of jealousy. Keep in mind that jealousy is usually the root of discord and resentment, which can lead to rejection.

> *"But Jesus said to them, "A prophet is not without honor except in his own country, among his own relatives, and in his own house"*
> *Mark 6:4 NKJV*

When time allows, read, study and search the New Testament for more detailed information on why people were jealous, showed resentment and rejected Jesus. I gave a teaser to encourage you to read your Bible. See what I did? (The above was from the book of Genia Moten that has not been written yet).

Jesus understands the jealousy that we go through. He sees the painful stages of resentment and, He is there to walk us through those hurtful times of rejection. The key is to be honest and tell Him how we feel. We are not smart enough to figure out everything. Life circumstances can be tough, but that's why the Word of God tells us to *"Cast all your care upon Him, for He cares for you" I Peter 5:7 NKJV.*

After Stephanie shared with Dana about how the therapist helped her to see things more clearly, she added, "Dana, I'm going to say something that you might not be ready to hear. You call it rejection, not being included. I call it protection. Sometimes rejection is God's way of protecting us from getting involved in things that are not meant for us. I kept blaming myself for not being invited and not being included in certain events. Then my therapist helped me to realize a lot of things. In reality, it was in my best interest."

The whole time Stephanie was talking, tears of hurt and pain were running down Dana's face. She dabbed at her face, blew her nose several times and then she looked at Stephanie and said, "I hear what you are saying Steph, but right now I'm still trying to process things. I just need to get through today. I like what you said. Don't get stuck. Don't stay in the rejection zone too long. I agree and you are right; I am not responsible for what people think or do towards me. But I am responsible for how I respond. So, thank you, Steph. Right now, all I want to do is get some rest." As Dana got up off the couch, she leaned over and hugged Stephanie. "You're pretty smart Sis" she said.

Stephanie said, "And likewise you are pretty smart too Sis. Trust me, it's going to be all right." They both hugged and chuckled softly.

Have you ever been where Dana was? You need time to process something painful before moving forward. In reality, you know that eventually everything will be all right, but you need time. I can't begin to tell you how many times I have been there. The song that is ringing in my head right now is, "I got a feeling everything is going to be all right."

Jealousy, Resentment and Rejection *turn them over to the Lord, then put on your dancing shoes.*

> *"Then David danced before the Lord with all his might"*
> *2 Samuel 6:14 NKJV*

So, I Danced!

Chapter 10
So, This Is The Reason I Dance

"Let them praise His name with the dance; let them sing praises to Him with the timbrel and harp" Psalms 149:3 NKJV

For Every Mountain
Kurt Carr Singers 2009

I've got so much to thank God for
So many wonderful blessings
And so many open doors
A brand new mercy
Along with each new day
That's why I praise You
And for this I give You praise
For waking me up this morning
That's why I praise You
For sending me on my way
That's why I praise You
For letting me see the sunshine
Of a brand new day
A brand new mercy
Along with each new day
That's why I praise You and for this
I give You praise
You're Jehovah Jhireh
That's why I praise You
You've been my Provider
That's why I praise You
So many times You've met my need
So many times You rescued me
That's why I praise You
I want to thank You for the blessing
You give to me each day
That's why I praise You
For this I give You praise
For every mountain You brought me over
For every trial you've seen me through
For every blessing
Hallelujah, for this I give You praise

When I think of all that God has done for me, I get excited. I feel, at times, like I am going to explode with excitement because He thought enough of me to grant me my heart's desires. No, God does not give me everything I ask for, but He blesses me in so many ways. *"For every mountain that He has brought me over and every trial He's seen me through, for every blessing, Hallelujah, for this I give you praise." This song speaks volumes to me.* **So, this is why I dance.**

When you were a child, did your parents ever say, "What do you want for Christmas? Make a list and put it on the table." Then you would feel excited while making your list. Not because you were going to get everything you asked for, but because of the feeling and anticipation: *maybe this will be the time you get what you asked for.*

When I pray, I get the same feeling at times. I pray believing that God will hear my prayers. The feeling and anticipation that maybe I will get everything I prayed for. My parents knew what was best for me when I made my Christmas list. So, they gave me what was best. But God knows what I need. So, He gives me what I need. Note that His answer may be yes, no, or wait. He never says maybe. He knows precisely when to give me (you) just what I (you) need. **So, this is why I dance.**

Have you ever been so overwhelmed by life that you felt like your back was against the wall? You look to the left, hoping to find the answer. Turn to your right to see if someone near you has some direction. No answer to the left. No direction to the right. What would you do?

This is what I would do if I were in this situation. Pray nonstop asking God to give me some direction. Then I put ice on my eyes because they were swollen from crying tears of sadness and tears of joy. I wash my face with cold water and throw the tissue box out after using the last tissue. For a moment, I was overwhelmed but now, everything is going to be all right. Since I like to dance, I would put on one of my old favorite songs, **"Don't wait until the battle's over and shout now."** *Shouting because God is working everything out.* **So, this is why I dance.**

In previous chapters, I talked about **David and Miriam and why they danced**. David danced "When David brought the Ark of God from Obed-edom's house to the place that he had prepared for it, there was great rejoicing". At the celebration, David danced before God in a way that his wife thought was undignified for a king (2 Samuel 6th Chapter). For Miriam, why did she play her tambourine and dance? The Israelites, when they saw what happened to the Egyptians who were pursuing them, (they all drowned), the Israelite's (which included Moses and Miriam) stood on the bank and praised God. They sang and danced. Then Miriam pulled out a tambourine and began to lead the women in singing, dancing and praising the Lord for what He had done for them (Exodus 15th chapter).

Now, let's talk about *why I dance*. Every time I have gone into surgery and woke up with the attendant's voice asking: 'Do you know where you are? Do you know your name? Do you know what year this is?' and several other questions and I can answer, this is why I give Him praise. I dance because of God's nonstop healing virtue flowing through my body. **This is why I dance for the Lord.**

Every time I have a family member connected to me by blood, chosen, connected through church or however else, tell me how they were spared, healed and delivered from danger seen or unseen, this is why I give Him praise. Also, for protecting me from dangers seen and unseen. **This is why I dance for the Lord.**

For every job I have worked, every apartment and home I have lived in, from the one to the twenty-plus pairs of shoes I have worn, for the meal of beans and rice to the salmon and strawberry salad I eat now, for the coat with two sweaters underneath to keep me warm, now to the fur and leather ones I wear, for every pleather to now my Coach and Dooney Bourke purses that I carry, this is why I give Him praise. For making ways out of no ways, for peace during my storms, for being a bridge over troubled waters including being a way-maker, problem solver and loving, forgiving, and keeping me - **This is why I dance for the Lord.**

> *"God never said that the journey would be easy, but He did say that the arrival would be worthwhile" Max Lucado*

Stephanie was sitting at the kitchen table drinking tea when suddenly she heard running upstairs. First in Dana's room, then in the hallway and finally down the stairs to the kitchen.

"Come on, Steph, you know what Sunday this is? It's Youth Day. You know what Aunt Trudy calls it," Before Dana could even get the words out of her mouth.

Stephanie said, "In and out day. The youth get us in and before you know it, we are on our way out." Both girls could not stop laughing.

"We are in trouble," Dana said, "Aunt Trudy has rubbed off on us."

Stephanie said, "You are right, we'd better hurry up. On the last Youth Sunday, we had to sit in the balcony because it was crowded on the main floor."

On the way to church, Dana said as she was driving, "For some unknown reason, I am excited about this morning's service."

Stephanie commented, "I know what you mean. I woke up like that – with a sense of excitement all around me."

"Also, I invited a few people. I'm not sure if they are going to come. I've been really concerned about them, even though I have my own issues. God has been speaking to me to let the past go. You'll see who they are if they come" Dana said.

Stephanie said, "Now, I'm really excited and I pray that they will come."

> **"The people who make a difference are not the ones with the credentials but the ones with the concern" Max Lucado**

As Dana was pulling into the parking lot she said, "See what I mean, we still have 45 minutes before service starts and the lot is almost full."

As Stephanie and Dana entered the sanctuary, there was a difference in the air. The song the Youth Praise and Worship team was singing ministered to their hearts immediately. The people in the pews were clapping as the singers sang. Some were walking around greeting each other and then there were those who were trying to find a place to sit. It was always great to see families come in together and fill an entire row. But this particular Sunday, the praises of the Lord began long before the service.

Numerous times I have been sitting in church before the service started, and while the music was playing throughout the sanctuary, I could feel the presence of the Lord. Several times I felt like I was sitting in the middle of a world wind and I felt His presence circling me repeatedly, engulfing me. Then suddenly surge through me. All I could do was say Hallelujah or lift my hands in praise. It's not uncommon to be sitting in our church and I look around or hear different people start personally praising God before the first hymn has been sung or, the opening prayer had been prayed.

The service started with Tina, a college student, welcoming everyone to the Youth Service. She told the congregation she was honored to be asked to participate in the service. She added that in three days she will be leaving to start her senior year at the university. Everyone applauded for her. Then something happened, before the first song was completed, the church went up into a Spirit of Praise and Thanksgiving. People who ordinarily would be sitting and watching were openly praising God.

"Praise Him with the timbrel and dance; Praise Him with stringed instruments and flutes" Psalms 150:4 NKJV. The organ, drummer and keyboard players were on one accord as they played a familiar upbeat song *"I don't know what you came to do but I came to praise the Lord."* The longer they played the song, the more people joined in. Some yelled out, "Praise the Lord." There was nonstop hand-clapping, patting of the feet, and tambourines beating. Suddenly, the Church Mother was up on her feet dancing for the Lord. The usher was no longer ushering people in; they, too, had joined in, dancing for the Lord. Everywhere you looked, from the children to the adults, they were dancing and giving God praise.

"Let them praise His name with the dance; Let them sing praises to Him with the timbrel and harp" Psalms 149:3 NKJV

Dana started crying uncontrollably in the Spirit and before she knew it, someone had put their arms around her. As she looked up, it was Bev. The two embraced, tears running down their cheeks. Bev asked for forgiveness. Suddenly, Dana did something she had never done. She started dancing to the Lord. First jumping up and down nonstop. Her arms were waving in the air, tears flowing as she cried out, "Thank you Lord." Then, Bev joined in, giving God praise and thanksgiving.

"You have turned my mourning into joyful dancing. You have taken away my clothes of mourning and clothed me with joy, that I might sing praises to you and not be silent. O Lord my God, I will give you thanks forever" Psalms 30:11-12 NLT

Stephanie knew, without Dana saying a word, who she had invited. So, she joined in with Bev and Dana giving God praise for all that He had done in their lives and, for the healing of two coworkers.

Dana whispered in Stephanie's ear, "Look." On the row behind them, it was their mother. She had finally come to church for the first time in almost two years with their Aunt Trudy.

As I close, I want to point out a few things. Stephanie completed eight months of therapy. The greatest lesson for everyone reading this book is: ***You/we have no control over people. There is nothing you can do to change how people feel or think about you. Nothing.***

Dana forgave Bev, who had excluded her from social gatherings and family functions, and invited her to church. Bev came. That's straight-up ministry. She put her hurt feelings on the back burner to win a soul for Christ (**clap, clap, clap, Amen**).

You have a gift that God ordained for you. Find out what it is by asking Him. The twins, Dana and Stephanie, had a compassion for people's well-being. They loved, cared for and listened to people, then they prayed for and with them. **When was the last time you prayed for someone? Really prayed for them.**

When God gave me the title "**So, I Danced**," and my editor suggested adding "**Before The Lord**," everything clicked (**Pastor Kim is such a wise lady**). **So, I Danced Before The Lord**. The more I said the more I could visualize, regardless of what I was facing. I danced.

So, when I hear songs like *"Take the Shackles Off my Feet so I can dance"* I picture shackles falling off me and I am able to be free and dance before the Lord. The song is not just an upbeat song; it's a ministering song. This song has a twofold meaning. One part is about my healing and the second part is regarding being set free and dancing before the Lord. In one of the lyrics, it says that regardless of how long I have been down, and even if I feel that all my hope is gone, I need to **"lift my hands, I understand that I should praise You through my circumstance."** This song is literally part of the book title, but in a different way. I want to dance and praise God no matter what I am going through. The gospel recording artists Mary Mary released an album in 2000 titled **"Thankful."** On the album, one of their hit songs was **"Shackles (Praise You),"** which ministered to me then and continues to minister to me even now.

> Take the shackles off my feet so I can dance
> I just wanna praise You (what you wanna do?)
> I just wanna praise You (yeah, yeah)
> You broke the chains, now I can lift my hands (uh, feel me?)
> And I'm gonna praise You (what you gon' do?)
> I'm gonna praise You
> In the corners of my mind
> I just can't seem to find a reason to believe
> That I can break free
> 'Cause you see, I have been down for so long
> Feel like the hope is gone
> But as I lift my hands, I understand
> That I should praise You through my circumstance

> Everything that could go wrong
> All went wrong at one time
> So much pressure fell on me
> I thought I was gon' lose my mind
> But I know you wanna see
> If I will hold on through these trials
> But I need you to lift this load
> 'Cause I can't take it anymore
>
> Been through the fire and the rain
> Bound in every kind of way
> But God has broken every chain
> So let me go right now

Hold Up. Before I complete this book, I need to testify. Keep in mind, as I am sharing, there comes a time in life when you sometimes have to dance in advance for what you think the Lord is going to do for you in the future.

At the beginning of 2024, a healthcare worker came to my home for my yearly visit as part of our insurance coverage. During the visit, I mentioned to the worker that my right leg kept feeling uncomfortable. Especially when I walked down the driveway to my mailbox. She asked several questions, checked my legs, and then suggested what it could be. Just so happens, the healthcare worker's field, when she is not doing home care visits, is cardiology. Before she left, I asked her to type what she told me into my phone so I wouldn't forget when I went to my primary care doctor.

Several weeks later, I had two different types of doctor's appointments. I let each doctor read what the healthcare provider said. One said I need to rest my legs more. I'm on the go a great deal. The other one went so far as to set me up with 10 visits to a physical therapist (PT) to strengthen my legs. (What?) At the end of all the pt's sessions, I went back to one of the doctors and said, "something is still wrong." I kept trying to get a doctor to understand that we need to take another look at my problem. Finally, to quote the one, "I'm only going to send you to a Cardiologist because that's what you think you need and that healthcare provider should not have put that in your head." (Really?)

Long story short. I was misdiagnosed. As soon as I met the cardiologist, the following was done immediately: a PAD (peripheral arterial duplex) - a study which screens for blockage in the arteries of the legs. An abnormal result suggests that one or both sides of the body have a detectable blockage.

On my visit, a heart monitor was put on me before leaving the office then followed by a series of stress tests. I ended up dealing with two types of heart doctors. One dealt with the heart and the other with the veins. The results of the test determined that there was blockage in both of my legs. (The healthcare worker was right). 100% in the right leg and 76% in the left leg. A decision was made to have surgery. I did not have leg surgery. The doctors had to do something else. Through more testing and the results from the heart monitor, it was determined that I would have a heart catheterization. (What in the world? Please help me, Lord). You want to know why I dance before the Lord? I went in for the heart catheterization and the doctors told my husband and two daughters, after the surgery, (I'm leaving a lot out) that I had 90% blockages on one part of the heart, 80% on another part, 30% here, 40% there. Lord, have mercy. There were two stents put in the heart for blockages. STOP. All I kept saying as the doctor was talking was, "I know a man who can make 100% healing in my body." God did it before and yes, He will do it again. This is only a fraction of what I went through right now. Only a fraction!!! The story is much longer. But my God is a healer.

If you know me, I like to stay busy and on the go. The doctors asked me to sit still for a bit, for my own good, no night air, cover my mouth before going out in the cold weather and just be still and heal. I had to learn to let people come and take care of me which was hard. When you are used to doing things for others and being the caretaker, it's a different story. Now I was the one who needed to be taken care of. After about four weeks, (and it was the holidays), I got to the point that I felt useless only because I wasn't able to help people. Yes, little ole me feeling that I wasn't needed.

Well, one night I had a dream and in the dream, I was a little overwhelmed thinking that no one needed me to help or to do anything. My daughters were having a gathering – not quite sure what it was for. Now, remember I said it was a dream. My daughters were running around trying to get things done and I really wanted to help but they wouldn't let me. I was in everyone's way. So, I went to look for a chair to sit down and get out of the way. But right in the middle of the dream, my granddaughter Imani came to me and said, "Nana, come with me. I have something for you." She took me into this small room, pulled out a garment bag from behind the door and unzipped it. Inside was a yellow Cinderella-type dress (I still feel the Spirit of God as I write this). She said, "This is for you. Put it on." She helped me get into the dress. "Slide these on." They were yellow pumps. The same color as the dress with a touch of gold. "Stand up, Nana. How do they feel on your feet?" she said. "They feel great" I replied. Then she said, "One more thing." She reached into a blue velvet purse-sized sack. "Bend your head forward." She then placed a beautiful crown on my head. Then she said, "Perfect. You're ready." Once I looked in the mirror, I started gliding around the room, praising and thanking God. Then suddenly, Imani was gone. Something startled me that woke me up. Wait. Not yet. I don't want to wake up yet. Did that ever happen to you? "I need to finish the dream attitude."

Later, as I sat and thought about the dream. The first thing that came to my mind was that the yellow dress represented the warmth of the natural sun hitting my body – healing from the sun but in reality, as I looked back at the dream, it was not the sun but the Son who was healing me. *Isaiah 53:3 says, "by His stripes we were healed. NKJV.* The shoes represented me walking by faith and not by sight. *For we walk by faith and not by sight 2 Corinthians 5:7 NKJV.*

The crown she placed on my head represented that one day, it will all be over and I shall wear a crown but while I am here, I must keep telling my stories, through my writing. Wow. What a dream. I still have work to do. I wasn't useless, but I needed to be still and heal. I like you, have a testimony that needs to be told, and someone is standing on the sidelines waiting to hear. Hear what? For me, God is a Healer. Come, let's give God some praise together.

I want to point out that when it comes to your health, if you think something is wrong, speak up. If at first the doctor or medical person doesn't listen, keep talking until someone hears you. God put that internal feeling inside of you for a reason. Speak up and speak out when it comes to your health.

In my closing. As I look at the lyrics of the two songs, *"Shackles"* and *"For Every Mountain"*, I am literally filled with a spirit of praise and thanksgiving. One song tells me that my shackles are gone, and I am free to lift my hands, dance and praise God. The other song, **(clap, clap, clap)** *"For every mountain You brought me over, For every trial you've seen me through. For every blessing Hallelujah, for this I give You praise."* Let's put a period right there. *Yes, this is why I dance.*

This book is about dancing before God for all that He has done. The two sisters in this book, could be you and me, interacting, talking and praising God in church and most of all forgiving the person who has excluded or rejected you.

So, do you have your dancing shoes on? Has God done anything for you to "dance for?" Has he healed you? Delivered you? Provided for you? Has He taken care of you? Protected you from dangers seen and unseen? Wasn't God there with you when you were rejected, hurt, disappointed, lost your job, experienced death, and you cried all night long? *I mean cried all night long.* You had no one to call who would listen to you. No one understood the pain that you were in. But God did. He understands what you are going through. So, go through your pain and suffering but don't get stuck there. Remember what I told you in the previous chapter. Talk to someone. Don't keep things bottled up. Let it out. If you call someone and they are not interested, then call someone else until you find someone who wants to listen to you, pray for you, pray with you and, cry. Cry as long as you need and *if you need to put the book down and cry, go ahead*) then focus on what His Word says, *"Weeping may endure for a night, But joy comes in the morning" Psalms 30:5b NKJV. Yes, your joy will come in the morning, but I don't know which morning.*

I don't know what He has done for you, but He has done a great deal of things for me. If by chance you can't think of anything God has done, then do me a favor: ***dance for me***. When you are dancing, dance like you have lost your mind. Why? That is what I would do for you. I would get my tambourine out, beat it and praise the Lord like I have lost my mind, just for you.

"Let them praise His name with the dance; Let them sing praises to Him with the timbrel and harp" Psalms 149:3 NKJV

"Praise Him with the timbrel and dance; Praise Him with stringed instruments and flutes" Psalms 150:4 NKJV

Inhale. Count to six. Now, exhale slowly. I pray that by the time you get to this page; this book will have been a blessing to you. It was a blessing for me. Each time I finished a chapter, there was a sense of closure in certain areas. I pray that you too are able to find some closure, healing and deliverance while reading this book. May the Lord richly bless you, my friend. Do you have your dancing shoes on? Are you ready? Come on, we've got something to do right now.

"Then David danced before the Lord with all his might"
2 Samuel 6:14 NKJV

So, This Is The Reason I Dance. So I Danced!

About The Author

author Mother Eugenia Moten

and spouse Elder Alfred Moten

Eugenia is the Founder of Teens Let It Out (TLIO) and the Single and Married Moms (SAMM), two support ministries. Teens Let It Out started as a writing and support ministry for teenagers and college students who needed spiritual advice and solutions to problems. As the ministry for Teens Let It Out grew, participants continued to stay in touch with Eugenia. She then saw a need and started conducting sessions on etiquette, manners, how to dress for interviews and public appearances. She is known for conducting sessions on "How to be a Lady from Head to Toe." Her sessions are conducted in the community and on college campuses. Eugenia's SAMM is a support group for mothers of all ages. The group serves as an outlet for mothers to share some of the difficulties of motherhood in a "no-judgment zone." She is a Certified Life and Grief Coach, and a Family Support Coach. Her support groups are based on the Bible scripture ***Psalm 121:1 KJV "I will lift up mine eyes unto the hills from where my help comes from, my help comes from the Lord."*** She is a published author of books and teaching materials.

She has been married to Alfred A. Moten, her friend and supporter, since April 1973. She is the mother of four children plus, five wonderful grandchildren and two great-grandchildren. She enjoys writing, conducting workshops/seminars in the church or in her community, interacting with people of all age levels and spending quality time with her husband and family. Most of all, when she permanently accepted Christ into her life as her personal Savior in 1976 in the Church of God In Christ (COGIC) in Harrisburg, Pennsylvania, she never looked back or regretted her decision. She is active and involved in COGIC in numerous church organizations, Mission Board, Prayer Group Mother, Church Mother, Evangelist/Missionary Board and she serves in different capacities in the Sunday School Department. Literally, without God, she could not have made it this far. Her daily quote: *"I will lift up mine eyes unto the hills from where my help comes from, my help comes from the Lord."* Upon completion of every one of her assignments, you will hear her say:

"So, Now What?" *And now*, "I Dance. So, I Danced Before The Lord."

Other Books by the Author

If The Truth Be Told, So Now What

Available via the author or Amazon (as released by the author)

Hello Sunshine Yay Sleepy Nights

Available via the author or Amazon (as released by the author)

Come On Now, You Got This

Available via the author or Amazon (as released by the author)

To contact the publishing co

Are you interested in writing or having your work (book, manuscript, poetry, how-to, autobiography/biography, etc.) published? Then reach out to the publishing company. We offer a range of consulting and publishing services.

The Crown And Cross Consulting And Publishing Co LLC
Attention: Kimberly Stratton – CEO and Founder
PO Box 952607
Lake Mary, FL 32795
Email: thecrownandcrosspublishingco@outlook.com

Notes

Notes

Notes

www.ingramcontent.com/pod-product-compliance
Lightning Source LLC
Chambersburg PA
CBHW080455170426
43196CB00016B/2810